Beware . . .

You are about to enter an ESCAPE BOOK — if you don't know what that is, here's the lowdown. An escape book is a puzzle book in which the unwary reader may become trapped for eternity—even longer than the most punishing Alcatraz jail term. It's an escape room in the form of a book. You can decide on your own path, but your route is often controlled by the solutions you give to the puzzles you encounter along the way. You must solve the puzzles to escape the pages.

Some puzzles offer alternative routes or courses of action according to your solution. Others invite you to calculate the next entry you should turn to. When this happens, you should check the "from" number at the top left to ensure that you came from the correct location. If you haven't, you should turn back and try again.

As befits an adventure set in the world's most famous and forbidding prison, you'll encounter rules, regulations, plots, tricks, and perplexing leads aplenty. And a few threats. Not all wrong solutions end the story. But some may have major unforeseen consequences further down the path, making you miss vital pieces of information or take wrong turns back into the maze of prison regulations and grim corridors.

In a prison you need to keep alert and when you're trapped inside an escape book, you must pay attention to everything you see. You'll come across clues that will be useful later in the escape adventure, so use the pages overleaf, which you carry hidden in your uniform, to make notes. You'll also need to master the code wheel on the book's cover (of which more later). If you are struggling, check out the helpful hints and clues (or even the answers) at the back of the book.

There is more than one outcome available as you try to exit the Escape Book. One represents freedom, and validation . . . others failure, and continued incarceration. Even humiliation at the hands of one of the Alcatraz guards. Only the most observant, keen-witted readers will work out the escape route that extricates them from the trouble they're in and results in a newspaper headline proclaiming heroic success.

▶ *These arrows direct you to your next entry.*
Now, all great adventures begin by turning the first page . . .

Your Notes

Use these pages to record clues, leads, and anything of interest you encounter. You may find they help you solve a later puzzle. Remember to keep the notes well hidden from the guards—or "bulls" as the inmates call them.

Notes and observations

▶ *If you have yet to begin your adventure, turn over the page.*

The Story

In this hard-boiled adventure, which takes place in the forbidding setting of U.S.P. Alcatraz, you take on the role of Scott Wilson, a wrongly imprisoned environmental campaigner. You've been framed as a murderer and sent to Alcatraz after the death of an FBI agent in a failed sting operation against the Wilderness underground environmental movement to which you belong.

It is 1962. John F. Kennedy is in the White House. But it's the height of the Cold War and the start of the Space Race with the Soviet Union, and there is great anxiety about national security. It's also a key period in the development of the nascent environmental movement, with Rachel Carson, author of the immortal *Silent Spring*, already hard at work campaigning against the use of synthetic pesticides.

As the book opens, you have just arrived in Alcatraz. During the raid on Wilderness HQ you received a head injury, and that, combined with the trauma of the event, has left your memory fuzzy and your thoughts unclear. At night, in your prison cot, you are troubled by vivid dreams and hazy flashbacks . . . You're left with a growing sense that you are racing against time to complete a vital piece of Wilderness work and get out of Alcatraz—some task!

In Alcatraz, the prisoners that surround you are infamous and often violent . . . and some just might be helpful. There is an almost impenetrable prison gang who—they say—knows all the prison's secrets and shortcuts, which guards can be trusted, and who can't. And you soon hear of escape plans, in particular that of Clarence and John Anglin, Allen West, and Frank Lee Morris, fellow inmates, who are already planning their famous escape of June 1962. Can you infiltrate these groups?

And what about Robert Stroud (the celebrated "Birdman of Alcatraz"), who was in the prison 1942–1959? Word is that Stroud left clues, hints, and suggestions of ways to escape . . .

Can you gather enough information, then piece together your memories to get out in time to save the day? You'll need all your wits about you.

The Code Wheel

Set into the cover of this escape book is a code wheel, which is an essential part of your equipment for solving some of the puzzles you will encounter. It features a series of windows, behind which are letters, numbers, colors, and a sequence of symbols. These can be used in a number of ways:

Color (input/output)

Letter (input/output)

Number (input/output)

Symbol (input)

You can find a digital version of the code wheel at:
https://www.ammonitepress.com/gift/alcatraz-escape-book/

In some puzzles you'll discover coded messages in the form of unintelligible notes or secret symbols hidden in the story. Using the code wheel, input your discoveries in the relevant input dial, then decode them by reading the relevant output dial.

▶ *Now it's time to turn the page and begin your adventure.*

"Get in there, boy." The prison guard shoves you roughly into the cell. "And shut your mouth."

"I am innocent," you mutter, turning toward him. "I have been framed. And I have to get out. I don't have time . . ."

"Heard it all before, buster." He slams and locks the door. "My advice to you is to accept what you are—and where you are." He laughs cruelly. "No one gets out. This is Alcatraz. Sooner you realize that . . . Look for blessings where you can . . . and follow the chalk back."

What does he mean? You try to catch his eye but he is gone. But you hear him say "Ciao," as he wanders off.

"I am innocent," you repeat. Aloud? Or in your mind? You're beginning to lose track, and feel so confused. It has been a whirlwind—your work at the Wilderness environmental group, the violent raid, then trial, conviction, and being sent down: to the forbidding high-security prison on Alcatraz Island. Average stay: eight years.

You lost good friends and colleagues. They say you killed an FBI agent in a brawl. But you took such a battering that . . . you're not sure. Something is wrong. Your memory is playing up. There are key elements of the story that are . . . missing. But you know that if you don't get out in the next few days something terrible will happen.

You look grimly around the cell. Cot. Folding table. Cold-water sink. Toilet. You stand and extend your arms. You can touch both side walls at once. You want to curl up into a ball but force yourself to take in your surroundings.

You see that on the table are three sticks of chalk, laid carefully in parallel. And on the sink—is it a toothbrush? Picking it up, you find it is a tightly bound roll of paper, which you unfurl. It's a fragment torn from a Bible.

Blessed are they which are persecuted for righteousness sake: for theirs is the kingdom of heaven.

Blessed are ye, when men shall revile you, and persecute you, and shall say all manner of evil against you falsely, for my sake.

Rejoice, and be exceeding glad: for great is your reward in heaven: for so persecuted they the prophets which were before you.

What could it mean? The guard said, "follow the chalk back," or was it "find the chalk at the back"? You can't be sure.

You try to puzzle it out. If you're going to become the first prisoner to escape from Alcatraz you're going to need all the clues and help you can get.

▶ *Take the third letter of the message you find. Follow its place in the alphabet to the next page.*

02 Misleading Ad

You stare at the ad for some time, but you don't seem to be able to get the letters to budge in your head.

You hear Alison's voice again.

"Follow the capitals, Scott."

The capitals? You wonder . . . But then you take a look back at the paper and you immediately see what she means.

▶ *Turn back to 87.*

03 A Tripped Alarm

You cut the red, orange, yellow, and green wires. As soon as you do, an alarm begins to sound. Your heart jumps to your throat.

You start running for the door. Back on solid ground you hesitate. Do you make for the coast or try and get back to your cell?

You start running toward the edge of the island, but you've barely taken ten steps before Jorgensen appears ahead of you.

"I'm a new officer," you say, "name of—"

"Yeah yeah. Running around at night. Setting off alarms. Confused identity, Wilson? You're gonna have a chance to get to know yourself in Solitary," he adds, before marching you back inside.

▶ *Turn to 62.*

Diverted

Almost at once the door bangs open and you jump slightly. You do your best to look as innocent as possible.

It's Officer Minnelli. "You alone here, boy?"

"The librarian Lévesque just stepped out," you say. The flicker in your voice gives you away.

"You're coming with me," he says. He taps you on the chest twice. This is meant to be a threat, and it is, but it also nudges something in your memory. The tapping. Last night. POPMEC362.

"One minute, I have a written request from the librarian to deliver an item . . ." You grab a random sheet from the table; luckily he does not check the sheet.

"Be quick," Minnelli says gruffly. He goes across to look out the window.

POPMEC362. It's not a book category. You look at pamphlets and catalogs. No. Magazines. You find it, and seeing that the bull is not looking, slip the magazine inside your shirt, where he cannot see it.

"Can't find it, Officer Minnelli. I'll let Lévesque know later."

You both head out.

▶   *Turn to 32.*

05 Fine Tailoring

In front of you are many pieces of fabric pinned together. There is a 7 scrawled in one corner, and a 9 in another. Four loose pins are at scattered locations across the table.

Above the fabric there is a single sentence: "Deliver me to the correct table." Looking around the room you notice each of the tables has a name. You read "CALF," then "WOOL," and finally "PINS." You have no idea what the correct table is. "PINS," maybe? There are lots of pins. But that seems foolish.

"Keep your eyes on the corners," a voice sounds in your head. Alison. She'd been training you for a recon mission when she said this sentence . . . "eyes on the corners" . . . Why are you thinking of it now?

► *You take the fabric to "CALF," turn to 76.*

► *You take the fabric to "WOOL," turn to 95.*

► *You take the fabric to "PINS," turn to 45.*

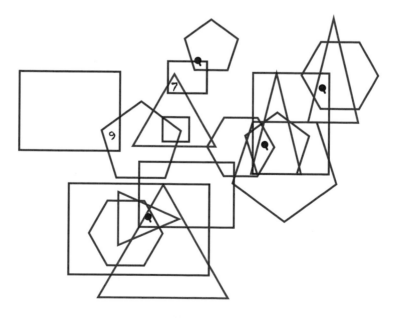

Gio

You arrange the 11 dice into lines on the step, before picking up a die, and showing Soprano a 6. He grins.

Several things happen at once. Soprano steps forward to clap you on the back, but as his hand reaches for your shoulder, another swings in front of your face. There's a sharp pain in your abdomen and you're doubled over on the ground. Your head smashes against the concrete.

With blurry vision you see someone standing over you. He's preparing to kick you in the head. You try to shout out, but no words escape your lips. It's like another dream. But you're not in Wilderness HQ, and this man is not a member of the FBI. This man is Gio. Guards wrestle Gio to the ground just before his foot makes contact.

As your consciousness begins to fade, you understand. Finally, you succeeded where Gio failed. Conte's men had been about to welcome you in. But now you're . . . now . . . Everything fades to black.

▶   *Turn to 34.*

A 7 of hearts. You draw the card on the book at the top of the tower and sit back. You have no idea what time it is—perhaps 3:00 or 4:00am?

You turn your attention to the last book, the one by the Menabonis. You flick through slowly, and finally on page 118 you find what you're looking for. A sequence of symbols annotated with words and sketches:

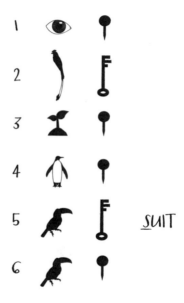

Over the following hours you review your scrap of paper, pulling together the notes and numbers you have gathered, and the answers to Birdman's puzzles. A plan materializes. Pins are directing you to rooms on the map, keys to keys. Your escape becomes clear.

▶ *Turn to 51.*

Snake Eyes

You take a note of the number.

A new officer, Washington, kind face and heavy Buddy Holly-style glasses, leads a group of you to the recreation yard to wait before your time in the mess. You're unsurprised to see another game in full swing. Now Soprano is at the center. You know keeping Conte's men onside is important, but your masquerade as Gio is only getting more risky.

The men are playing on the bottom two steps. You walk up. And as if he can hear your thoughts, Gio himself is standing there. He's staring at you. With a new menace in his eyes. He knows . . . you think. You look away quickly.

"Careful, Scott," you hear Alison say. She's morphing into half-companion, half-conscience. You shake her away and focus on the game being played. Today, it's dice. Soprano is explaining the challenge.

"Find a way of arranging these dice so they make two lines of five dice, and three lines of three. The total shown on each of the longer lines should be double the total on each of the shorter."

Simple enough. You count 11 dice on the steps. Soprano is speaking again. "Use exactly four of the six numbers. Take the sum of each shorter line, then take away U. Tell me what you got."

You nod. Gio makes a move forward, but Soprano brushes him away. Gio snarls. Soprano gestures to you. You move over and give your attention to the dice.

▶ *Turn to the number Soprano asked for.*

09 Drowsy

You write down the answer, 9, still unsure what any of these bird-book letters and numbers means or how they'll help you. You need to get off this island, to the hidden evidence and to stop the bill. Part of you wonders if these puzzles are simply a distraction, but they seem to be your only option. You're hoping and praying a plan will fall into place, but from your sickbed, it feels further away than ever. You sigh and let sleep wash you into a fitful slumber.

▶ *Turn to 72.*

10 A Useful Tool?

Having fitted the hexagons into their board, you are looking for 👁. You wonder about arrangements of furniture in this shape. Or whether you might find the mark on a wall or area of window grill? You begin to look at the bookshelves. And sure enough you find the mark on a copy of *Bewick's British Birds*.

And you know you must be on the right track because the back part of the book is hollowed out. Inside you find a cardboard code wheel device that appears to convert symbols to letters and colors. *This is the code wheel in the cover of this book.*

What's more, some of the symbols were used on the hexagons. Then the door opens. You rush back toward the main desk.

A tall, skinny man, thick mustache, small glasses glinting in the light. "Hello!" he says. "Who are you? What the heck are you doing here?"

▶ *Turn to 75.*

Click

Five turns counterclockwise. Click. The heavy door shifts slightly.
You push. You are through. They say no one escapes Alcatraz.
They're right. Till now.

You've been picking the brains of some great minds. The escape
plot of Morris, West, and the Anglins got you out of your cell and
delivered the raft you're carrying. Amazing. They said Morris was
super-smart.

You convinced Conte's crew that you were Gio, and they delivered
the means of getting out of the main prison house.

Now you have the steps of the escape scheme laid out by the Birdman
of Alcatraz. You have the numbered map and the six pieces of
information he gave you.

You stand with your back to the door, heart thumping. It's here
that two of the plans intersect, you think. In Conte's plan, for Gennaro,
it is Omega, "the last place you should try." But it's also the first step
in the Birdman's plan, 16 on the map. Conte's crew have given you
what the Birdman lacked—a way of getting through this heavy door,
into the chapel and associated rooms.

On to the next stage. At the foot of the chapel stairs, you search for a
yellow key. Search and search—remember it must have been hidden
years ago. Finally you find it, wedged into a crack in the woodwork of
the old stairs, and well concealed with paint.

Next? Look up room number 8: the telephone room. You go quickly
up the stairs, through the chapel. The yellow key opens the door.
It occurs to you in passing that Conte's plan was focused on getting
Gio this far—presumably to call information out.

Next step is room number 9.

▶ *Turn to 88.*

12 Annotations

You drop off *Notes of a Native Son*, then set off to deliver a book that was not included in the librarian's puzzle. It's a copy of Charles Dickens's *Great Expectations* to Clarence Anglin. You note that he has Cell 152—same row as yours.

The trolley is piled high with books, which shake a little as you wheel, or is that you? You're trying to keep your nerves in check.

Turning the corner onto Michigan Avenue, one of the wheels sticks, sending trolley and books tumbling to the floor. You are quickly down on your hands and knees, picking the books up.

Something catches your eye. A book has fallen open. First you find a sheet giving a Morse code key. You pocket it. Then a page with pencil markings. You realize the book is *Great Expectations*, and peer closely. Is something hidden within?

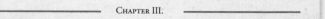

CHAPTER III.

It was a rimy mor●ing, and very damp. I had seen the damp ly●ng on the outside of my little window, as if s●me goblin had been crying there all night, and using ●he window for a pocket-handkerchief. Now, I saw the d●mp lying on the b●re hedges and spare grass, like a ●oarser sort of spide●s' webs; hanging itself from twig to twig and blade to blade.

▶ *You find the hidden message, turn to 35.*

▶ *You can't find anything, turn to 55.*

Lime Point Lighthouse

You paddle toward Lime Point Lighthouse. You make sure you keep the evidence well out of the water. You feel like singing, looking toward the city and the Golden Gate.

A small boat meets you. Hank from the Wilderness is there and helps you on board.

"You have it?" He says, greedily opening the envelope. "It's all here! You're a genius, Scott, you pulled it off!"

"We had to hide it somewhere that no one, literally no one, would look," he murmured. "Nowhere like The Rock itself."

You look around. The sky is blue. The bay is beautiful, the hills are green. As the fellow says, it's a good day to be alive.

▶ *Turn to 53.*

14 On Michigan Avenue

FROM 1

"Benvenuto, Gio," you whisper the words aloud. What could that mean? Benvenuto is Italian, for "welcome," you believe . . . But you're no Gio. Have you been mistaken for someone else? Or is this a prison threat you don't understand yet?

You jolt alert as a guard begins rattling the cell door.

"Mess hall," he barks. "Get on it. Up!"

You exit the cell. Two guards escort you down to ground level and along a deserted corridor between cells. From behind, one says, "Didn't expect to be walking along Michigan Avenue, hunh? And toward Times Square?"

"What do you mean?" you ask.

"A fish, hunh? Don't-you-know-anything? We get to walk Broadway, Park Avenue, Michigan Avenue here in Alcatraz—just like the Big City," he says.

"Shut up, Minnelli!" says the guard in front. "No more questions. No more talk."

"What's eating you, Beckett? Why you so sore?"

You look around uncertainly. "Where is everyone?"

"In the mess hall," Minnelli says. He shows you his wristwatch: 4:27pm. "We're late."

Officer Beckett growls and leads you into Times Square, where you're told to wait.

▶ *Turn to 71.*

"Runaway"?

15. Page 15 has an article about life preservers. Could that be it? You add it to your store of information. Something's going on with Morris and men on the corridor. A plot? You thought you heard "escape." The raincoats.

Then the message on the pipes seems to have led you to this magazine. Life preservers? You think of the waters all around The Rock.

At the same time, there's the "Birdman" books and the puzzles you found. Are they connected to Frank? Or to the librarian? He seemed to want you to find the prison plan.

And there's Conte and his men. Gio. They seem to be plotting their own way out. In the next cell, Morris has started playing "Runaway," the Del Shannon hit you remember from the Billboard Hot 100 last year. You whistle along. It helps you think.

▶   *Turn to 87.*

16 Symbol 16

Looking up E in the index, you find written against it the letters SCAPE to spell "Escape." Underneath is a drawing, which seems to show a bird with a man's legs and—in front of it—six footprints. You take a note of the number.

Six footprints . . . to ESCAPE? But look for them where?

"How many books with symbols have you just collected?" Alison's voice gives you a start. It sounds like she's right behind you.

Seven books, the first holding a map of the prison, and six left. You think of the six books and wonder . . . Six puzzles, six answers, six steps to an escape.

▶ *Go to 84.*

Evidence

You click in the numbers 3-7-1-6, and the safe eases open. Inside is a thin folder, which contains just 20 or so pieces of paper. It's scarcely believable: being thrown in Alcatraz, the raid on HQ, the loss of so many Wilderness members. Everything happened for these pieces of paper.

You flick open the folder and read the first few lines. ". . . find evidence of the illegal and highly destructive activities of a cross-partisan farming lobby, which has to date included the use of poisonous pesticides and political machinations of the most corrupt kind—bribery, intimidation, and murder. The lobby is staging a large-scale land grab and we urgently need . . ."

You safely tuck the papers back into the folder and stand. Time is running out—judging by the darkening of the sky you have less than an hour to get to the pick-up point out in the bay and hand this evidence for the *Mail* over to an ally.

You make your way to the water's edge. Keeping the folder safe, you untie the raft and lay it on the water. You remember from the *Popular Mechanics'* life-preserver article instructions about fitting a device for inflating by mouth. You find that and it takes a few minutes—minutes you don't have—to inflate the device.

Once it's ready it almost bobs away when you look back for a moment up at The Rock with a laugh in your heart. So, no one escapes from Alcatraz? You catch the raft just in time, climb gingerly into it, and orient yourself, ready to start paddling.

You know where you're heading. The papers have told you . . .

▶ *To paddle toward Treasure Island, turn to 85.*

▶ *To paddle toward the Lime Point Lighthouse, turn to 13.*

▶ *To paddle toward Angel Island, turn to 101.*

18 "Do the Twist"

FROM 64

"Come on baby, Let's do the twist . . ." You hear Morris's voice from his cell next door. "Take me by my little hand and go like this." Another coded message, you wonder?

Officer Joyce pounces. "Shut up, Morris. You know singing's not allowed."

The tune of Chubby Checker's hit carries on without words, Morris playing it on his accordion. Every night there is music "hour," 5:30 to 7:00pm, when music's allowed in the cell block.

You sit listening to the song, trying to make sense of all the different pieces of information: "Gio," Conte and his men, clues that might add up to an escape plan, books about birds. You also remember Alison dancing to that song, how she could twist right down to the floor . . .

Afterward, the silence is sad. You listen to a mournful clanking in the pipes. Ancient plumbing? Or a pattern? It repeats—soft knocks followed by louder ones. With careful pauses between what must be sections of message.

You grab a pencil and note these down with dots and dashes:

► *You try converting this message. Turn to 58.*

A Musical Vision

You note the color. The list is getting long—and confusing. What could these different notes mean in the bird books? You're determined to make sense of them.

But you need to sleep. At night you hear scratching or scraping noises from time to time. Rats? You think. You sleep deeply, wake up humming. A tune has lodged itself in your brain. A defiant earworm, refusing to move. Last night's dream is crystal clear—and all the stranger for it.

You are sitting around a table, surrounded by the Wilderness members. There are seven clicks and then everyone starts singing. You can't quite hear the words, but you know you are surrounded by music.

There is something you need to do. Then your colleague Alison turns to you and sings words that are crystal clear: "Find the evidence, Scott, Take the evidence, Scott, Send the evidence, Scott, Stop the bill, Scott."

She turns away from you and you look down on the table at the map below. This time there is no blurry mass, but instead a map of Alcatraz. In the bottom left-hand corner, a compass with four letters, clockwise, but the East E is an I and the West W a G. There are seven clicks.

You stop humming. A new horror is dawning on you. Not only have you been framed and stuck in Alcatraz to rot, but there is evidence that needs to be found and sent, and a bill to be stopped. How are you—trapped here—going to achieve any of that? Time is short, you have the *Mail* article to prove it. You have to crack this code, get out of here, and prevent a catastrophe out there.

▶ *Turn to 42.*

20 Bald Eagle

You look up Bald Eagle in the handbook. Seems you're on the right path straight away. Next to the entry is the symbol ❱. The same one you noticed on the cover.

The Bald Eagle page is stuck to the next page and there is a small hole in the paper, through which colors are visible. Carefully holding apart the top of the pages that have been stuck together you pull out a hand-drawn map—the layout of the main prison block. (*The map is at the end of this book.*)

Did the librarian intend you to find this? Or did he share the book without realizing it had been doctored by someone? Someone planning an escape. Or wanting to help other people plan their own escape . . .

You think again of Conte and the men in the mess hall . . . the business with "Gio" . . . could they be behind this?

Whoever it is, it's good news . . . as is the code device. You're making progress, if slowly.

But where to keep them? It's not safe in the cell. There's always the risk of a "shakedown" when one of the bulls searches the cell. You decide you'll carry the code device and map with you all the time, inside your shirt or pants.

Your spirits are a little better. You sleep deeply, without dreams. The next morning in the mess hall you get stuck between a giant Scandinavian they call "Big Lars" and Winston, the man from the yard steps. Conte and Soprano and others seem to be eyeing you with interest.

▶ *Turn to 104.*

Back to 136

So, you'll need to add the lighthouse to your escape. One quick blink to the *San Francisco Mail* team to let them know you're on your way. Easier said than done, perhaps. You're still lost in your plan when the hospital orderly Desmond walks in. You jump up quickly.

"You should be resting," he says. "You're still in recovery."

"I'm—busy," you try to protest.

"No dice. You're going to your cell," he says. You take a step toward him and then you're struck by a brainwave.

"Give me one moment," you say. "There are some books I have to look at." One of the Alcatraz raincoats is flung down on a chair. You pick it up. You're grateful to see Desmond sit down for a moment.

"No rest for the wicked," he says, and sighs.

You duck into the Ornithology section, gather the books marked with the Birdman's symbols, and hide them inside the coat. If you're ever going to decipher his instructions, it's going to be tonight.

You turn back to Desmond, holding the raincoat in front of you, and follow him to your cell.

▶ *Turn to 68.*

After lunch you're back to deliveries. You encounter your neighbor Frank Morris being taken back to his cell. He looks right through you, his eyes dead. He is struggling with an armload of possessions, books, and papers—has he been given library permissions?

Round the corner, the corridor is empty, and you see a book on the floor. It's Mark Twain's *The Adventures of Huckleberry Finn*. It seems to have loose pages, which slide out when you pick it up. Intriguing.

The obvious explanation is that Morris dropped it. You pick it up and take a close look. At the front is a handwritten dedication.

Surveying the loose pages, you realize they have been removed and collected at the back. You scan the pages for information, but find nothing. In the bottom-right corner each page is marked with a number.

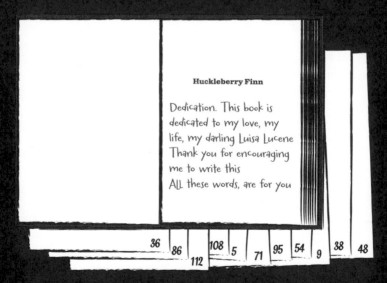

You suspect a hidden message of some kind. But who could it be intended for? Why would Morris be carrying it?

▶ *Work out the message and turn to 83.*

To the Library

You move away from the fence with a slight nod to Conte. The library. A direction, a destination. Although you're not quite sure how you'll get to go anywhere new. Life in Alcatraz is a strict rotation of cell—mess— work— mess—cell. But you'll need to find a way, and fast.

Conte and his men seem to be focusing on you. Sending messages. But why? Your best guess is they're testing to see if you're this "Gio." The words you overheard seemed to say he wasn't going to identify himself. You'd best play along, you think. There could be plenty to gain from allying with Conte and the group. Protection? No one knows this jail better than them. Even help getting out?

There are three sharp rings of a bell, and you all trail into the mess hall and lunch.

▶ *Turn to 59.*

Doubts

You'd hoped that the plan would ease your panic, if only a little. Now you're here, you're filled with doubts. How did the Birdman plan this all in so much detail? You remember he was researching a prison history book, but still . . . And how can you be sure nothing has changed since he made the plan? He got moved out in 1959, three years ago . . .

Inside Alcatraz, doubts are your enemy, too. If you have a chance you have to take it. Your recovering memory . . . you have a sense that as a journalist and campaigner you're an old hand at going where you're not wanted—and uncovering secrets. If you have a plan, you have to try it. To get off this island, find the evidence, and get it to the *Mail*. It's better to try—even if you fail and end up in Solitary—than rot in this cell with the land deal going through..

Footsteps alert you to the approach of a bull. You push the books, notes, and puzzles under the covers of your bed and climb in with them at your feet. And feign sleep.

▶ *Turn to 70.*

25 Hospital Reading

FROM 38

"When will they let me off St. Helena?" you shout.

You're stringing it out for as long as you can in the hospital. You are genuinely ill for the first couple of days and then you try delusions. "I demand to see Mr. Balcombe!"

"A little reading of the newspaper will help the prisoner back to a sense of who and where he is." Jean-Louis picked his time carefully, when the least aggressive orderly, Desmond, is on.

"Yes, OK."

You know this can't go on. You know D Block Solitary is waiting. You know the future is grim. But at least you didn't fail completely. It's a comfort to see the newspaper clipping and what Jean-Louis has achieved.

The End

SAN FRANCISCO MAIL

LAND DEAL AXED

ROLE OF FARMING LOBBY EXPOSED; STATE OFFICIALS ACCUSED

ALCATRAZ LIBRARIAN MAKES SHOCKING STATEMENT, SHARES TOP-SECRET DOSSIER

"PESTICIDES POISONING OUR LAND"—"SAVE OUR WILDERNESS," SAYS SPOKESMAN

A top-secret dossier shared with the Mail has exposed a possible political scandal behind the proposed sale of 200,000 acres of northern Californian wilderness. The documents were forwarded to our offices by an Alcatraz inmate. An anonymous spokesman for an underground pressure group calling itself the Wilderness declared, "Stopping this immoral land grab is a great moment for our state."

The deal would have seen the land divided up among landowners and farmed intensively using the most modern methods. A state spokesman said "I am saddened by this development," but would not comment further. Some have accused the state of selling off future Californians' birthright. But a scientist allied to the purchasing group, Dr. Karl Boschwitz, was adamant that the deal was needed to feed future generations. "Why would we not take advantage of the benefits modern science offers to agriculture?"

Continued on page 2

"PRISONER FRAMED"— ANONYMOUS

A second dossier shared anonymously with the Mail claims Alcatraz inmate Scott Wilson has been framed because of his involvement with attempts to stop the land grab.

Continued on page 3

DEADLY "SILENT SPRING"

The Mail has seen an advance copy of marine biologist Rachel Carson's potentially sensational new book Silent Spring, due to be published this fall. It warns of the dangers of pesticides' poisonous effect on the environment.

Continued on page 31

FRANNY AND ZOOEY TOP OF THE PILE

JD Salinger's novel Franny and Zooey, one of the top-selling novels of 1961, remains at the top of the most-wanted lists in our bookstores.

Continued on page 7

TRIBAL COUNCIL APPROVES ELVIS ROLE

Elvis Presley has been inducted into the Los Angeles Tribal Council by Wah-Nee-Ota after the success of the King's role in Flaming Star, which opened just before Christmas.

Continued on page 12

26 Back on Broadway

FROM 77

After breakfast you make it to the library. A few words' debrief with Jean-Louis. Gio, he tells you, is in Solitary. D Block. Later you head out with the trolley.

Back on Broadway, a voice startles you. "Hey, books! Where ya goin' next?" You see Conte, relaxed as ever, reading a magazine.

You pause, lean on the book trolley. You wonder, is there information coming about where to go next?

"Ha! Prime Hustle, they're calling it . . . Just catchin' up on the reviews of *The Hustler*. Pool and petty crime. Can't beat it, eh? Ya like Newman, Books? Some ladies I used ta know say I looks a little like him . . ."

Strikes you that the handsome Conte is not far wide of the mark.

You look around for clues. These are intended for "Gio," but the man you think is Gio is locked away in Solitary in D Block. Looks like you've won that particular battle.

Whatever's going on, you need all the information you can get. You feel your sleeve where you have hidden the numbered prison map and code device. You check out the scene for clues.

▶ *Turn to the number you think they're directing you to.*

Beckett opens the library door and nods brusquely. You hurry in. The door clicks loudly shut.

You find you are alone. Where is the librarian? The library is beautifully quiet. You had claimed familiarity with books, so you think you'd better look busy.

Thinking of the birds in the yard, you wander over to the ornithology section. Tucked on a shelf you find a folder marked "research." Inside there are seven hexagon tiles and a library card with a message.

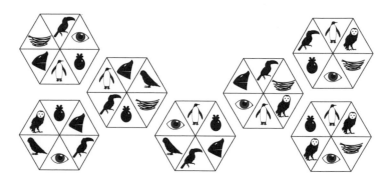

ALCATRAZ PENITENTIARY LIBRARY

Fit 6 around 1, no rotating.
Where hexagons along straight line, symbols match.
Fit hexagons into board. Look for bottom-center symbol

▶ *If you think it is 🍐, turn to 61.*

▶ *If you think it is 👁, turn to 10.*

▶ *If you think it is 🦉, turn to 86.*

The Green Door

You walk confidently through the green door into a bustling kitchen scene. Minnelli is standing at the other end of the room. He catches your eye and nods. You breathe a sigh of relief.

Then suddenly someone is shouting at you to cut carrots and before you know it you're attacking a sack full of carrots with a very blunt knife.

The morning hurtles by. As you're being taken from the kitchen to the mess hall for lunch, Minnelli catches you,

"In the recce, find Ricci," he says as he walks ahead of you.

You see him speaking to Gio a few moments later. Your rival must have found the right answer, too. So, the battle continues. It won't be a pretty—or even fair—one, you think. Judging from the look Gio gives you, you'll need to be on your guard. You join the line for lunch, with the yard, Ricci, and carrots circling round your head.

▶ *Turn to 93.*

29 The Wharf

FROM 90

You make your way over to the wharf. Try as you might you can't go completely unseen. In the distance you see a guard who looks like Jorgensen on patrol. You silently thank Stroud again for the uniform part of the plan. It's saved your bacon. You nod and raise a hand and the guard—Jorgensen or someone else—waves but doesn't approach.

When you arrive, the sky is turning pink. At the far end of the wharf is a small hut, and your heart leaps. You run toward it. The roof is a little too high to reach, but even from here it looks more or less flat. You're unsure where the evidence might be hidden, but no matter.

You unstrap the raft from your back and roll a barrel over toward the hut. Over the next hour you move the barrel around the hut, searching every inch of the roof's surface. Nothing.

Your excitement dies away. The sky grows lighter and lighter. You've hit a dead end. You climb down off the barrel and make your way back toward the island.

But at the top of the wharf, you're met by Jorgensen.

"Taking a trip?" he asks. You say nothing.

"The only place you're going is Solitary. A few months' vacation in D Block."

▶ *Turn to 62.*

The Real Gio

After lunch you make for the library, but Officer Minnelli cuts across your path. "This way, buster," he grunts.

You join a group of prisoners, and together you're led outside, and over to the New Industries Building. Inside the Clothing Shop you watch the rows of men bowed over their work. Something sparks in your mind. Outside. In Frisco. You were a journalist, wrote about the exploitation of prisoners who were forced to work for 50 cents a day.

Minnelli's voice cuts across your thoughts. "Sit," he blurts. You're unsure why you've been pulled from the library, but you swallow your questions. He stalks off. You think you hear him say, "Ciao, Gio," as he exits. You nod.

You look at the table ahead of you, and see some pinned fabric and a note. This must be another challenge—Conte's doing. You try to look calm. You can feel the eyes of the room on you.

You return to the puzzle, but before you can begin reading, the door opens again, and Minnelli marches a different man into the room. He's short, in his 50s, with a pot belly and balding head. Small round glasses. The guard sits him at an identical table, same pinned fabric and same note. As he exits again, you hear another, "Ciao, Gio." This man nods, too.

You look at "Gio," and realize that this must be the Mafiosi accountant in the flesh. As you thought, Conte and his men are unsure who is who. If you want their help, and you do, you're going to need to convince him that you're Gio, and that this man is an imposter. To do that, you'll need to solve this puzzle, and quickly.

▶ *You get to work, turn to 5.*

31 Trouble

"31," you say.

"Yes, got it," he says, "I see now. Good work, son."

But then Music Hour is interrupted by a visit. No less a figure than the Warden.

"Wrap up that racket, Morris. Officer Joyce tells me he's suspicious of events in the corner. I see you there, Wilson.

"Joyce warned me about you and West, Morris. He's unsure what you're up to. So this is what's happening . . . You're all being moved. It's a shame Joyce is not on duty to see this. But Officer Washington is on duty and will handle it, won't you, son?"

As he turns away in his rage, the warden doesn't notice a scrap of paper slip out the bottom of his pants . . . a hole in a pocket, you assume. You slip your foot over the note, and when no one's looking, pick it up to stash it.

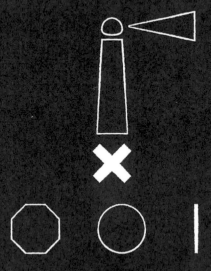

► *Turn to 57.*

What's Cooking?

You follow Minnelli through the long grim corridors of Alcatraz and through the mess hall to the kitchen. As you enter the room you are hit with a wave of heat and scent that is overpowering.

You arrive at a workstation in a secluded corner. You keep your eyes down, enough to avoid eye contact, but not so much that you miss that Gio, the accountant, is stationed at another workstation behind your own.

"Holy cow," you think. You're in deeper with Conte and his men than you intended.

Minnelli points at the station. There's a written message and three vials. He points to the door to your left, and says "Red," points to the door behind you, and says "Green," and then points to the door to your right, and says "Blue."

As Minnelli steps away, you turn your eyes to the table.

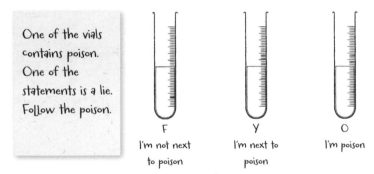

One of the vials contains poison. One of the statements is a lie. Follow the poison.

F — I'm not next to poison

Y — I'm next to poison

O — I'm poison

You look at the guard and he runs a single finger along his throat. You don't know if it's directed at you or about the poison. You don't want to find out.

▶ *To go through the green door, turn to 28.*

▶ *To go through the red door, turn to 39.*

▶ *To go through the blue door, turn to 67.*

33 Utility Corridor

You focus your attention on the panel beneath the sink, which is slightly misaligned. You manage to pull it from the wall. Morris must have been working at it. Was that what the noise you heard was?

It reveals a hole big enough to slide through. You stop. Listen. A cough here and groan there. A man—Morris?—is talking in his sleep. Go. You pick up your notes and tools and push yourself through.

After some uncomfortable squirming in the dark, you emerge on the other side of the wall. You are standing in the utility corridor, which runs directly behind your cell. You climb up the pipework, quiet as you can.

As you ascend, you find a space between the top of the third tier of cells and the roof. It must have been where Morris and the others set up their workshop—it's a treasure trove of items—raincoats, scattered tools, an electric drill made of what looks like a vacuum motor. There are raincoats welded together with glue and heat to form a makeshift life preserver and raft.

Just like the magazine described. Genius to use the raincoats. Must have Morris to thank for that. You breathe a sigh of relief. You locate some light rope and set about strapping the raft and life preserver to your back. It's heavy and in your drowsy state you sway a little under the weight as you climb back down the pipework.

You hear some scraping in the wall behind you, and your heart quickens. Is Morris trying to come through from West's old cell? He'll need to work at the opening, you think. You tie the final rope and push on along the utility corridor quiet and fast as you can, praying Morris isn't on your tail.

▶ *Turn to 94.*

Prison Hospital

You wake with a start to find someone standing over you. Gio? Whoever it is takes a step closer. And you flinch, begin to panic.

The man smiles and places a glass of water on your bedside table. Slowly your memory returns—the punch, the fall, your face. It makes sense. The dream you just had, that's another matter.

In the dream, you are sitting at a table with the Wilderness. You look around, and everyone looks up. You look up, too. On the ceiling you hear a single click. You look back at the table and there is a map. No one is talking. You look at Alison. She looks up, and you do too. Another single click.

You reach for the map and suddenly it's far above you. You pull it down. Another solo click. Another click. Everyone looks at you. You look at them. They look up.

Then everyone reaches for the map. It's far above them and they pull it down to hide it in their coats. You look at them. They look at you. They look up. There is one click.

That's all you can remember. Your head feels scrambled, but one thing is clear. They were looking at you. You are important somehow. Just you.

You shift and try to sit up. The man—he must be a nurse or medical orderly—says, "Gently now, take your time." Then your memories click into place. The evidence is hidden and you're the only one to know its location. All of it—the evidence, the bill—you're the only one who can stop it. And you're in a hospital bed, in prison, on Alcatraz.

▶ *Turn to 99.*

35 Tree of Letters

"Raincoat." You ponder the word. A warning for the exercise yard, perhaps? But why is it hidden in a book? You sigh and head back to the library.

Back in your cell, you are tired, tired, tired. But you know you can't rest. You look at the code wheel device. A puzzle led you to it. It was obviously left for someone to find.

Your pulse quickens. Are there the elements of an escape plan lying around, waiting to be picked up? There are clues in the library and clues linked to Conte. And then *Great Expectations*. How can these all be linked together? The sets of clues seem separate.

You pick up the book Jean-Louis handed to you. *Birds of the World*. Odd. Why would he think you'd be interested in birds? You notice a symbol ❯ on the spine. The symbol looks familiar.

On page three there is a sketch of a blossoming tree. As you peer closer, you realize the tree isn't growing leaves but letters. Below are four numbers, with phrases after each.

1. GO NATIONAL
2. HOARSE BLACK
3. RED CRESTED
4. CAGED YELLOW

Below there is a line of instructions. "Find these words in the leaves."

▶ *Find the extra letter.*
Use the code wheel to follow this to the next entry.

You look him dead in the eyes then open your mouth: "Good friend, for Jesus' sake forbear, to dig the dust enclosed here. Blessed be the man that spares these stones, and cursed be he that moves my bones."

There is a long silence. Then the warden rises, walks around to you, and slaps you on the back. He's laughing.

"A Shakespeare-head!" he shouts, pointing at you.

You nod. "The words written on his tomb."

"That's no job, Wilson." But he's softened. He leans on the desk, which groans a little under his weight, and kicks his legs out ahead of him.

"I worked with books," you manage to say, trying to keep your voice steady. He doesn't respond. He watches you and then returns to his chair behind the desk and flicks through the papers in front of him.

"We always need people in electrics—" he says.

"It's the tragedies that get me," you say. "The sense that it was always coming."

He looks at you, seriously, then his face cracks into a smile. "I just like the violence myself . . ." then he winks.

"Our librarian's asking for help. Just got rid of Prisoner Ricci. Need to look into that . . . On your way, Officer Beckett." You stand and follow.

▶ *Turn to 44.*

A Rude Awakening

A kick to the cell bars jolts you awake. Two guards—Beckett and O'Brien—are standing above you.

"You looking for trouble?" O'Brien has a broad grin. "You're headed to Solitary. A new reality. On your feet."

You obey. What point is there in fighting? You've failed to get out of the cell, and you lost concentration at the crucial moment. You flush with shame.

▶ *Turn to 62.*

A Failed Attempt

The Coast Guard delivers you back to The Rock. You are shivering, teeth chattering. Only one good thing: You managed to keep the evidence out of the ocean.

It's time for Plan B. As arranged with Jean-Louis. You collapse. You're raving. Talking garbage. Also, you're genuinely sick after your long exposure to the waters. The medic finds that you're running a sky-high temperature.

Jean-Louis times his rounds so he's in the hospital when you arrive and manages to distract the orderly for long enough for you to drop and kick the evidence under the bed. Two minutes later you're being strip-searched. You see the librarian bend down unobserved and pick the envelope up from under the bed.

▶ *Turn to 25.*

39 The Red Door

FROM 32

You make a move toward the red door, and out of the corner of your eye, you see Minnelli move involuntarily.

You can see that your move has surprised him, and it makes you question yourself. Perhaps things are not quite as they appeared. You return to your table.

▶ *Turn back to 32.*

40 The Staircase

FROM 73

You unlock the door, and step into the lighthouse. A long, winding staircase stretches upward. You run through the plan as you take the steps. From the light outside, you think it must be 3 or 3:30am. You have just a few hours until your cell will be discovered empty and The Rock will be in lockdown.

You still need to send out a blink to the *Mail*, find the evidence, and make it to the meeting point. At the top of the staircase you find another lock to get into the control room. You can almost see the minutes slipping away in front of you.

▶ *Turn to 47.*

In the Recreation Yard

Some "Park Avenue" residents are loudly playing dominoes. Several men are wearing the heavy standard-issue raincoats though it's a sunny day.

"DIVEBOMBERS!" A voice shouts. You see a seagull sweep in on the wind and its droppings splatter across a group of the men. Wearing the coats suddenly makes sense.

"If we could jump on the tail o' the winds like them birds . . ." A tall inmate is beside you at the top of the steps that run along one side of the yard. "Winston," he says, "outta New Orleans." You both greedily take in the view—sky, bay, Golden Gate Bridge, the city on the shore.

You're piecing together any clues that come your way . . . And you have to start making things happen, you decide.

Down the steps you approach the fence. A handful of Broadway prisoners are blocking the way, but seeing you come, they move. Filippo Conte nods at you pointedly and appears to indicate the fence directly behind by flicking his head.

He walks away from you backward for perhaps seven or eight steps. There's something unusual on the fencing.

▶ *Take your message and follow each letter to its place in the alphabet. Add them to find the next page.*

42 Cell 138

The bull yells: "B! Everybody out! Work details!"

You notice Morris is not there outside his cell, 138. You take a couple steps forward and look in. "Frank?" you whisper. But no reply. There's a scuffle down the line and the bull yells "Everybody still!"

You look in Morris's cell. Any chance to pick up a few more bits of information, you think. The cell is empty but there are a few unusual things about it. You make a mental note.

You think of the map you have hidden in your pants. You've identified your row of cells there. What you see here suggests to you a location on the map and where to head next for further clues . . .

. . . Officer Joyce is looming over you—"Get movin!" he says, pushing you in the back.

There's not the time to go there now, but you know where you're gonna be heading when you next get a chance.

▶ *Turn to 60.*

43 The Right Frequency

You jolt awake in panic. You fell asleep? How could you have fallen asleep?! You stand up.

Your dream floods back—you were trapped, locked in, but the message came clearly through.

You are in the room with the members of the Wilderness. This time you're not sitting at the table with them, but outside somehow. You realize that you're inside a safe. There are muffled sounds, and then six clicks. You strain to hear their conversation and, like tuning a radio, you suddenly find the right frequency.

"Our informant will deposit the evidence at the agreed location on Alcatraz Island tonight. We'll hide it right under their noses. No one will look there. Scott will boat there and then swim to the location tomorrow, and we'll be able to deliver the material to the Mail well in advance of the bill's intended release. All clear?"

Everyone in the room nods. In the safe, you nod, too. There are muffled sounds and then six clicks. You push at the door, but you can't escape. You hear muffled sounds and then six clicks. There are footsteps outside the door.

You open your eyes. You don't want to experience that again. But it is good news. You'd had your suspicions, of course, but now it's clear: the evidence is here, on the very island where you have been imprisoned. The evidence is on Alcatraz, and you are the only one who knows where it is. Better get moving.

▶ *You put together the plan, turn to 90.*

Last and First

Officer Beckett opens the heavy door beside the chapel that leads from the front offices to the main prison block. You watch him turning the key in the lock. "What are you looking at?" he asks. "Planning an escape?" You nod.

"Look at this door," he says. "This is the last place you'd want to try breaking out. Sure, you'd be the first to escape." He swings the keys round his hand. "But trying it would be the last idea you ever had."

Just then a man hurries up from the offices. "Morning, Gennaro," he says. "You'll be needing Gennaro's services when you get a haircut. Not too often, though . . . once a month!" He laughs cruelly.

▶ *Turn to 27.*

Pins

You decide to ignore Alison and go with your gut. You prepare yourself to walk to the "PINS" table, but she is insistent.

"Keep your eyes on the corners," she says again. In your mind, of course. Then, "What are the pins cornered by?" You stop. That last sentence was never spoken by Alison. It's something else, some hidden part of your brain trying to communicate with you. You decide to listen to it.

▶ *Turn back to 5.*

46 The Maltese Falcon

FROM 79

There are bulls everywhere. Minnelli, Beckett, O'Brien. Robertson, Joyce, Jorgensen. "Keep moving! Stop dawdling! What're you looking at?" You don't get a chance to stop till you're in C Block. Suddenly nobody's looking. You slip your hand down your pants and extricate the package. A voice from one of the cells—"Enjoyin' yourself?" A huge blond inmate is eyeing you.

You ignore him and turn away, desperate to see what Gennaro gave you. Inside is a slender tool with a bent, rounded end. It's wrapped in a paper of sorts.

"Hey, books! Where is my *Red Harvest*? I order it up." Look at the paper later, you decide. You stuff the tool and its paper back down the front of your pants.

"That one was missing on the shelves," you lie. You always bring a few spare books on the trolley. "I got this. Probably better." You offer him *The Maltese Falcon*.

He sticks out his bottom lip, nods, and takes it. "*Tack*, books," he said. He extends a hand: "Sven Rasmussen. Outta Stockholm via New York."

▶ *Turn to 97.*

Silent Night

It is so quiet everywhere. You can feel the silence all around you.

You need to disable the alarm system. You know you'll need to cut some wires, but which ones?

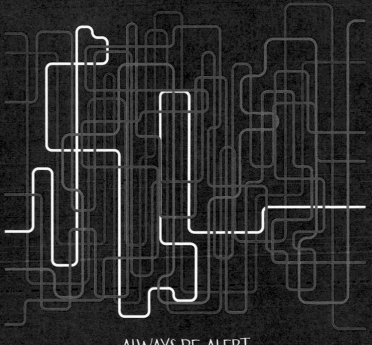

ALWAYS BE ALERT

After considering the system for a moment, you reach in and cut:

▶ *The yellow, blue, and red wires, turn to 80.*

▶ *The orange, green, and pink wires, turn to 78.*

▶ *The red, orange, yellow, and green wires, turn to 3.*

48 | A Librarian's Code

You nod and take the book. Jean-Louis disappears behind a bookcase, then reemerges, wheeling a small trolley piled high with magazines, pamphlets, and books.

"First task is to do the rounds today," he says, pushing the trolley toward you. You catch it, and nod.

"Deliver these books to the cells," he says, evidently reading the confusion in your face.

"How do I?" you ask. There's a pile of books and a list of prisoners, but no way of connecting book to cell.

"Ah yes!" Jean-Louis exclaims. He rustles around on his desk and finds a typewritten list. Letters and numbers. Some sort of code.

CATCH-22	JOSEPH HELLER	
Notes of a Native Son	James Baldwin	
A Raisin in the Sun	LORRAINE HANSBERRY	
REBECCA	Daphne du Maurier	

ALCATRAZ PENITENTIARY LIBRARY

Hank Mortensen, Cell 245

Filippo Conte, Cell 103

Frank Morris, Cell 138

Aaron Johnson, Cell 127

---

831 – QV
721 – BP
542 – OV
301 – FA

"You'll be able to work that out," he says. "It's a relatively standard librarian's code. 14." You nod. "And I gotta be getting back to this." He turns away and, with his back to you, adds, "maybe drop off *Notes of a Native Son* first."

Your mind is racing. You didn't know there was such a thing as a librarian's code. But you can't ask for help or your cover will be blown. You smooth out the paper on top of the books and look closely.

What's a librarian's logic? you wonder.

▶ *Find your destination from the first two digits of the cell number.*

The Cell Door

The tool from Gennaro. The lock on the cell door. You bend down and set about trying to pick the lock. The mechanism is unlike anything you've seen. You've years of experience from your work with the Wilderness of listening at safes, and easing your way through locked doors and over high fences. This one won't budge. You take a moment's rest.

▶ *You continue picking the lock, turn to 37.*

▶ *To go to the ventilation panel under the sink, turn to 33.*

50 Deep Dreams

You rouse yourself groggily, trying to shake off the last remnants of a dream that lingers in your subconscious. Then you stop yourself. There was something. Something that you can't put your finger on, something just out of reach that just might be worth remembering.

In your dream, you are seated at the same wooden table surrounded by members of the Wilderness. People are speaking and now you can hear the words: "Create a valuable expedition." They're talking to you. Urgently. Something is happening in six days.

The clock ticks, but erratically. There are three ticks, then a long break.

You look again at the map. Someone points at it. They speak, too. "Catch a veiled enemy," they say. They lock eyes with you. You nod. They tap three times on the table.

Just before the footsteps, one final message: "Car, airplane, van, escape." The word "escape" rings in your ears as the door is barged open. Again, there is a fight, punches, and again you're on the floor. You feel blood run from your ear down your neck. Then darkness. And silence.

The dream dislodges something in your memory: a government bill: imminent, dangerous, devastating. To be passed in six days, you bet. Or six days from then. So, four days for you. You better get a move on.

▶ *Turn to 69.*

A Way Out

Birdman's clues can get you out of the building, you think. You map out a route as birds start to chirrup above you. The day is waking, and you haven't yet gone to sleep.

You'll start by going through the door to the chapel (map number 16) and finding a yellow key.

In the area of the chapel you'll go to the telephone room (number 8), followed by the storage room (number 9).

There you'll get a green key (following the first letter of Hearts on the code wheel).

Finally, in the projection room (number 7) you'll use the green key to open the windows. And climb down the building . . .

You sit back and sigh. So there it is.

▶ *Turn to 24.*

Tangled Up

Your hand reaches for an end of the rope, and you gently start to pull. Almost immediately you feel the rope catch. You put the rope back down again and scratch your head.

You look over at the guard. He's staring in your direction, a brutal grin etched across his face. He's enjoying this.

You turn back to the rope, determined to not give him what he wants, and look again at the tangled mess.

▶ *Turn back to 102.*

53 Lying Low

You meet Hank on Marina Green, by San Francisco Bay. You're well disguised, lying low. You pull the hat down over your eyes and settle into your trench coat.

"Think Philip Marlowe, Bogart, *The Big Sleep*," Hank joked with you when he gave you the disguise. Now he brings you coffee, donuts, some cash, half a bottle of bourbon, and a couple packs of smokes.

And a copy of the *San Francisco Mail*. He gives you a wave and a brief, respectful bow in passing but does not risk stopping.

You feel like leaping for joy, like jumping up and doing the Twist, but instead you sit quietly and read.

The End

SAN FRANCISCO MAIL

LAND DEAL AXED

LAND DEAL AXED
ROLE OF FARMING LOBBY EXPOSED
ALCATRAZ INMATE—"HERO OF ENVIRONMENTAL STRUGGLE"—SAID TO BE INVOLVED IN FOILING PLOT

A secret dossier shared with the Mail has exposed a stunning political scandal behind the proposed sale of 200,000 acres of northern Californian wilderness. The documents were forwarded to the Mail's offices by an Alcatraz inmate. An anonymous spokesman for underground pressure group the Wilderness declared, "Stopping this immoral land grab is a great moment in the history of our state."

The deal would have seen the land divided up among landowners and farmed intensively using the most modern methods. A spokesman for the state said "I am saddened by this development," but would not comment further. Some have accused the state of selling off the birthright of future Californians. But a scientist allied to the purchasing group, Dr. Karl Boschwitz, was adamant that the deal was needed to feed those very people in the future. "Why would we not take advantage of the benefits of modern science as they can be applied to agriculture?"

Continued on page 2

ESCAPE FROM THE ROCK?
Helicopters were circling and Coast Guard vessels crisscrossing the bay as the authorities searched for escaped inmate Scott Wilson. A prison spokesman denied the claim. "There's been no escape. One prisoner drowned in the Bay."

Continued on page 3

DEADLY "SILENT SPRING"
The Mail has seen an advance copy of marine biologist Rachel Carson's potentially sensational new book Silent Spring, due to be published this fall. It warns of the dangers of pesticides' poisonous effect on the environment.

Continued on page 31

FRANNY AND ZOOEY TOP OF THE PILE
JD Salinger's novel Franny and Zooey, one of the top-selling novels of 1961, remains at the top of the most-wanted lists in our bookstores.

Continued on page 7

TRIBAL COUNCIL APPROVES ELVIS ROLE
Elvis Presley has been inducted into the Los Angeles Tribal Council by Wah-Nee-Ota after the success of the King's role in Flaming Star, which opened just before Christmas.

Continued on page 12

54 Cards

In the recreation yard before lunch you notice a group of men in the corner of the yard. It appears to be a game. Sat at the table is Ricci. He has a pack of cards in his hand, and five cards placed face-down on the table in front of him. You watch as men step up in turn to guess at the hidden hand. Ricci explains the rules:

"There are five hidden cards, each showing one of either 10, J, Q, K, A. You can make five guesses at these cards. My cards. If you get the right suit, in the right place, I'll place a red token to the left of your hand. If you get a right suit, in the wrong place, I'll place a gray token. A white token means wrong suit, wrong place. If you get the right value, in the right place, I'll place a red token to the right of your hand. If you get a right value, in the wrong place I'll place a gray token to the right. A white token on the right means wrong value, wrong place."

Your head swims as you try to take this all in. Ricci adds another line, now looking directly at you. "Take the ends away from the middle." The wheel again, you think.

Ricci shuffles the deck and starts the game again. You watch for a few moments, as four men make their guesses. For each, you note Ricci's responses.

Perhaps there is a way to use these tokens to help you reach an answer? Can you find Ricci's hand in what has already been guessed?

▶ *Follow the middle number to the next page.*

Few Expectations

You stare at the page for a few moments, but you can't make any sense of the pencil scribbles. And begin to doubt you ever will—so much for great expectations, you think. But the symbols and words are swimming in your mind. You think of your friend Alison. She was always good at puzzles.

Her voice rings clear in your ear. "Don't look at what they show you Scott, look at what they don't."

She always knew what to say. You slip *Great Expectations* off the trolley and look again.

▶ *Turn back to 12.*

You make your way toward San Antonio, on the other side of the island. But try as you might you can't go completely unseen. In the distance you see a guard who looks like Jorgensen on patrol.

You silently thank Robert Stroud again for the uniform part of the plan. It's saved your bacon. You nod and raise a hand and Jorgensen waves but doesn't approach.

By the time you reach the cave, the sky is turning pink. You edge down to the water and find the cave flooded. These discoveries make you a little uneasy, but you push on.

You slip off the raft you're carrying, leave your notes and tools outside the cave, and slip into the water.

You spend what feels like hours swimming along the cave's floor, searching for any irregularities, any holes, any hidden evidence, but your search reveals nothing.

You reluctantly come to accept that you have made a mistake and swim up to exit the cave. Perhaps head to Sing Sing and look there?

Standing above you is Jorgensen. He holds your notes and tools in his hand. The raft is at his feet. He looks you dead in the eye.

"I'm a new guard," you try, "name of . . . John Kennedy. Just lost my . . ."

"Hokay, let me think . . ." He laughs. "Lost your . . . ID pass . . . in a flooded cave? Hahaha." He goes on: "Confused identity, Wilson? You and me, we're gonna take a walk to Solitary. D Block. You can get to know yourself in there."

▶ *Turn to 62.*

Next Door

The plan is to move you, Morris, and Allen West into empty cells in A Block.

You have a hunch from looking into Cell 138 earlier that Morris is up to something in there. And so you're glad you managed to get into Washington's good books during the course of the day.

When the Warden has safely departed, you ask: "Maybe you could just swap us around, Officer Washington? No need to shift us so far?"

It's a long shot, but amazingly it works. You get 138 and Morris gets West's cell at 140. West gets your cell, 136. They're both pretty pissed about it, which just makes everyone more riled up and suspicious.

▶ *Turn to 100.*

Time Will Tell

Dots and dashes—the best you come up with is the Morse code. You remember the Morse code sheet you found slipped inside *Great Expectations*, which was bound for Clarence Anglin. Using that gives you POPMEC362.

Not much use? Time will tell . . . Answers and codes are mounting up . . . you decide to start keeping a list on a scrap of paper of any information that may prove useful. But for now—sleep.

▶ *Turn to 50.*

59 The Warden

As you rise from a sloppy lunch of beans and coffee, you hear your name and number being called. You check the hall to be sure none of Conte's men are watching before you identify yourself. Luckily, the coast is clear.

"Wilson. AZ1888?" one of the guards—or "bulls" as you've heard the inmates call them—asks as you approach. You nod. "The warden's callin' for you, boy."

You swallow. The beans haven't settled. You feel sick. You follow the bull from the mess hall, down Broadway, and toward the main entrance.

The bull knocks on the Warden's door, and the Warden calls "Enter!" You stand before him. "Tell me about your experience, son," he almost bellows. "Not murdering and the like," he chuckles, a gold tooth glinting in his mouth, "but your occupation."

You look around the room and see your opportunity. Perhaps there is a way into the library after all. But this man will need buttering up. You'll need to say something to get him onside . . .

▶ *Follow your instinct to the next passage.*

60 Step by Step

Back in the library you're looking for books and magazines on Jean-Louis's list—a 1933 *Abbott's Monthly*, a 1944 *Esquire*, *Double Indemnity*, and a couple other James N. Cain novels . . . You detour to take another look at the Birdman books you've secured in Ornithology.

You pick up the one marked with the ♟: *Migration of Birds* by Frederick Charles Lincoln. Must be another puzzle here, you think. But you can't find anything. Finally, you hold the book up to shake it and find a puzzle drawn on tissue-thin paper and slipped down the book's spine.

You see a sequence of triangles scattered across the page, with collected instructions below.

Place 1 to 11.

1 is directly below 2 and directly left of 3 (which is above 4)

5 is directly below 6 and right of 7 (which is above 8)

9 is directly right of 4 and above 11 (which is below 5)

8 is directly below 9 and directly right of 10 (which is above 11).

You get to work.

▶ *Follow the red triangle.*

Symbol E

Having fitted the hexagons into the board, you're convinced you need to find ⬤. You look all around, but you can't see it anywhere. Then you look back at the board and see your mistake. You decide to try again.

▶ *Turn back to 27.*

In Solitary

In your solitary cell, you feel the weight of your failure. So much for the escape plan. You're done—stuck in Alcatraz now.

You failed to get the evidence to the *Mail*. Without that, the bill will definitely go through. The land is lost, and all the work you and the Wilderness did has gone to waste. All for nothing.

You slump on the hard floor and put your head in your hands. In the distance, from one of the other cells, you hear a voice.

"Scott! I say Scott! I'm coming for you, old boy!" Gio, or should we say Sir George, is almost screaming with glee. You lie down, rest your pounding head on the floor, and face your new reality.

▶ *Turn to 96.*

63 | Feeling Ropey

Your hand reaches for an end of the rope. As it does, your eyes jump through the mass of tangled fibers and you almost immediately find a knot. Your hand falls back to your side.

You feel utterly helpless. Not only are you stuck in Alcatraz, but you're stuck sorting piles of matted rope, and you can't even do that.

With a sigh, you return to your desk, and the knotted rope.

▶ *Turn back to 102.*

64 | Stockpiling?

After the Clothing Shop, you're hurried back toward your cells, Officer Jorgensen and a new bull, Joyce—all 6ft 7in of him—much in evidence.

You're dragging your feet, keeping an eye on your neighbors. One is Morris, who ordered up the *Catch-22* book. You think you hear the other one murmur something. It sounds like, "Escape on?"

Joyce looms over him. "What did you say?"

The prisoner holds his hands up as if in surrender. "Capon," he says, "Tape's on. Play on." Looks like he's playing with Joyce.

Joyce looks at him menacingly before turning to the other prisoner. "Morris, what's that you're carrying?"

"Replacement raincoat."

"Why do you need that? Didn't I see you carrying one last time I was on duty?"

"Not me. No sir."

The other prisoner intervenes, "Must have been me, Officer Joyce.

When was you on duty last?"

"Shut up, West. I know it was Morris. You boys stockpiling? What for? I'm keeping a close eye on you two, and the Anglin boys, this whole goddamn row of cells. You, too, Wilson."

▶ *Turn to 18.*

Sour Dreams

You jolt awake. You are covered in a thin layer of sweat and you're breathing heavily. The sounds of your nightmare linger around you. Shouts, cries, gunshots. You lie very still and try to recall your dream:

You are seated at a wooden table in a dingy underground room, surrounded by Wilderness members. They speak in hushed, serious tones: making a plan. They keep looking at you. You keep nodding. You can't hear what you're agreeing to. There is only white noise.

There's a map at the center of the table, but it's only a blur. Someone to your right says something important to you—a number, a location, a name—you can't be sure. You lock it away in your memory.

Footsteps on the stairs. Panic. Rolling up the map and tearing documents down. Someone swallows something. The door bursts open. Men. Guns, masks, camouflage.

You are knocked to the floor, hear a high-pitched scream. You don't know if it's in your head or outside. There are kicks, punches, shots, blood on the floor. You try to stand up but your head is like lead and you can't get up. There is silence. You sink into the darkness.

Then you wake up, here. Waves of emotion hit you: grief, fear, panic. You search your memory for the thing you hid there, but can't find it. So much is missing: the maps, the plan, the names, the faces. To get out of here you're going to need to find your way through that white noise.

▶ *Turn to 102.*

66 The Dead of Night

You wait for the guards to finish their 1:00am check of the cells. You know you have a five-hour window, before the 6:00am check, to get out of the prison, to the lighthouse, and off the island. No time to waste.

You look around Cell 138. Just like 136. You feel at home! But there were a few key clues you noticed about Morris's cell. Your heart is pounding. "Breathe, Scott." Alison says. You listen and take in a gulp of air. Need to get moving.

You ease out of bed, and ready yourself for the start of your plan.

▶ *To walk to the cell door, turn to 49.*
▶ *To walk to the ventilation panel beneath the sink, turn to 33.*

67 The Blue Door

The answer is blue, you're sure of it. You gather yourself to leave, and then you hear a voice in your ear.

"Look again, Scott." It's Alison. You shake her off. You're about done with her interjections. But she's not done. "Pride comes before a fall."

You sigh deeply. She can be infuriating, but she is right. You return to the vial and the puzzle.

▶ *Turn back to 32.*

68 Dominoes

"Hey-yay Baby, I wanna kno-oo-ow if you'll be my girl . . ." Music Hour, and Morris is at it again.

"Come on, Frank, no singing." Officer Washington takes a gentler approach. "They tell me you're real smart, so you should know better."

Morris carries on with the song, accordion only. There's that scratching and scraping sound again, but Washington seems to ignore it.

"What's that about Morris?" You ask Washington. To make conversation and get him onside.

"Yeah, IQ of 133." You chat jazz a bit more . . . Coltrane, Thelonius Monk. He's on about Eric Dolphy again. "'It's magic,' as the song says." Then he pulls out his newspaper.

"You know what, Wilson, you might be able to help me, son. See this puzzle here? It's got me stumped."

"Sounds like you should be asking Frank here." He laughs.

He shows a grid with numbers. The four corners of the grid are circled. Twenty-eight dominoes are depicted next to the grid on the table.

"Have to draw the dominoes on the grid so each shows once and only once. Find domino totals in the corners. What they add to?"

▶ *Follow the number you find to the next passage.*

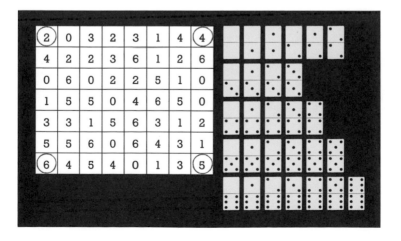

In the library you turn to today's delivery list. Top of the list is *Diseases of Canaries* by R. Stroud. At the first chance you get you wander over to Ornithology to take out the seven books you'd left hidden there.

You pick up *A Coloured Key to the Wildfowl of the World* by Peter Scott. It's marked with a symbol on the spine 👁 .

You're not yet sure why all of these books have been marked in the same way, or how the books are connected to the code wheel you're holding in your hand, but you're determined to find out.

You flick open the book, and on the inside cover you find a small puzzle lightly sketched. Curious to find where this will lead you, you grab your pencil and get to work.

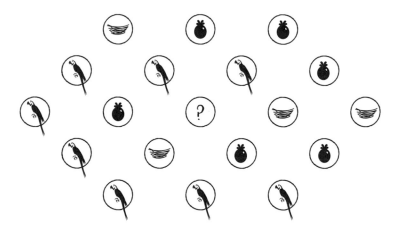

▶ *Follow the question mark to the missing passage.*

"You Save the Day"

Sleepless in Alcatraz. You feel sick to your stomach. Your head aches. All you can do is push on.

Lie low, you think, await your chance. In the mess hall next morning you sit at the far end from Conte and his crew, watching them warily. You're certain they don't see you. But the men nearby, including Big Lars and Sven, look threatening.

In the library, though, Jean-Louis is a friendly face. You decide to risk everything, give him the lowdown. You're going to make your move tonight. He looks at you wildly. No details how, you say. The less he knows the better.

You share the Wilderness plan. There is a package you still have to locate to be found and delivered. You talk for a moment about what lies beyond the prison block, the island layout . . . lighthouse, beaches, wharf, caves. . .

"Strange," he says, "caves are named after other prisons. Sing Sing. San Antonio. Someone having a bit of fun, at some point." Is this useful? You feel impatient.

"Listen," you say, your throat dry. "You support the work? The project?" He nods. "This may work, it may not. I need a Plan B. If I track down the package and get caught, I'm gonna pretend I'm mad or sick or whatever it takes to get into the prison hospital. There. If possible, I'll tell you where it is, or give you what I know. If I fail, you save the day."

He opens his mouth, closes it, and nods.

▶ *Turn to 81.*

Beckett leaves you with Minnelli, who is still talking. Another guard approaches him.

"Did ya see this, Minnelli? Your family's active!" He is waving a newspaper.

"My family? What you saying, Jorgensen?"

"The family. The Mafia. Cosa Nostra."

He throws the paper at Minnelli, who drops it. He's distracted by swearing at his colleague. For a moment you see the headline and first few lines before he gathers it up.

MOB ACCOUNTANT JAILED?

Anthony LaGuardia   **March 13, 1962**

Alcatraz Penitentiary may soon be hosting royalty—Mafia royalty. Latest word on the street is that an unidentified prisoner due in at the San Francisco, CA, jail is in reality the Mob accountant known only as "Gio." It is believed that the man known as Gio is in fact English nobleman Sir George Alexander.

Continued on page 13.

Minnelli tucks the paper under his arm and pushes you toward Jorgensen, who leads you into the mess hall.

▶ *Turn to 92.*

"Good to Go"

You come awake gently. Silence. You feel free, joyful. But then the whitewashed walls of the hospital room press in around you once more.

"Wilson. Prisoner AZ1888?" The loud voice of a medical orderly hauls you back to the present. His badge says DENZEL DESMOND. He takes your pulse and listens to your heartbeat, shines a light into your eyes, and asks question after question. "Feeling clear-headed? How many fingers am I holding up? Where are you? What's the President's name?"

"I'm feeling A-OK," you lie. "Three. Alcatraz . . . in the sanatorium. President John F. Kennedy." You seem to satisfy him. But you're feeling groggy.

"Prisoner Wilson, you are good to go. As far as the mess hall, anyway. Take 'er easy today."

▶ *Turn to 77.*

73 The Lighthouse

FROM 88

From your pocket you take the scrap of paper you picked up when it slipped from the Warden's pants outside the cells. The moon is out and her light touches the path and the waters of the bay. You see the glittering lights of the city in the distance. Soon.

Navigating toward the lighthouse, you keep a close eye on the ground. There are cracks in a paving stone that seem to make an "X." Grass grows in the cracks, making it more visible. "X marks it," you hear Alison say in your ear. You're glad she's with you for this.

You hold the note between your thumb and forefinger, finding a gentle indentation in the paper that tells you it's been held this way many times before. You wonder briefly why any guard would need a reminder like this. And why would the Governor, who dropped it, be carrying the paper for him? You recall what Jean-Louis said about the old guard, and the Governor's protectiveness toward him. His forgetfulness and the Governor's uncharacteristic attitude are a good thing for you. You decide you'll have to put it down as an unexplained bit of luck.

Your eyes flick between the note and the building as you search for a connection, but you're drawing a blank. You reach for Alison. "Watch these visuals," she says back. It was always her invite to the dance floor. You think briefly of her doing the Twist again. Shake your head. It's not helpful now. Though you wish you could be dancing. With her. Somewhere safe . . .

You concentrate on the lighthouse above, and let Alison's words show you the way.

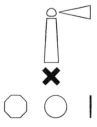

▶ *Follow what you see to the next passage.*

74 Listen Up, Scott

You pocket the report and the ad. "Listen up, Scott." To what? You wonder. You scour the page again for more clues, but there seems to be no message to listen for, yet.

You set about gathering books for today's trolley, and as soon as you have reason to get close to the ornithology section you retrieve the next of Birdman's texts: *The Waterfowl of the World* by Jean Théodore Delacour. It's marked with a small symbol ⟩ . You place the book on its spine and watch as it opens to an illustration.

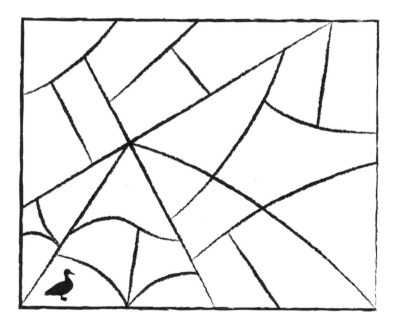

Below are some notes: "Three types of flower to be planted: red, pink, yellow. No flowers of the same type can be planted next to each other. Follow the bird."

Jean-Louis comes down the ladder and finds you staring at the image, perplexed.

"These could be from the Birdman's gardening phase," he says, pointing at the garden design. "He chose specific plants and flowers to diversify the bird life here." Jean-Louis smiles absently. You know that the Birdman's reasoning was a little more complex. You pocket the book with a plan to find the garden later.

▶ *Turn to 54.*

A Friendly Face?

"Wilson. Newly arrived. Well, yesterday. I worked with books before. So the Warden told me to report to you . . ."

"Ah. Jean-Louis Lévesque," he says, suddenly calm and extending his hand. "Librarian. Good timing. Got rid of Ricci. More trouble than he was worth . . ."

Your eye falls on a tall pile of typescript on the desk and you look enquiringly at the librarian. "Ah," he says, "I am writing a history of Alcatraz rock and of the prison."

"Outside," you say, "in the world, I read a lot of history . . ." Your voice trails off. You realize how your memory loss means there's so much of your past life you're unsure of.

He turns away, hands you a volume. "Would you like to borrow this book to read?"

▶ *Turn to 48.*

76 Calf

FROM 5

You finish your calculations and land on "CALF." You take it to the correct table. For a moment you feel elated—you glance over to see the man you identified as Gio is still working on the problem. He eyes you uneasily as you walk past his table.

▶ *Turn to 64.*

77 Mealtime

FROM 72

Officer Washington collects you. "Quite a blow you took, son. You mendin' so soon?" He is older, has a kinder voice and face than his fellow bulls.

You exchange a few words in the grim corridors. Seems he's a jazz fan, and the names and dates come back to you from your battered memory.

"Gotta try the new Eric Dolphy album," he says. Adds ruefully, "If you get a chance . . ."

You make it to the mess hall in time for breakfast. You look warily around for Gio. Nowhere to be seen. One of Conte's men steps in front of you as you are about to sit down. A quick look across the table at Conte himself is enough to settle you. His face is frozen in a fixed smile that fails to conceal his ruthlessness.

No one really smiles in Alcatraz. But at least he's outwardly calm. All seems to be going OK. Another of his henchmen gestures to you to sit on a different table, behind you. Turning, you see a couple of his men moving away to leave you space.

You look at the bowl, plate, pitcher, two spoons, and a fork. At first you think it's a mistake, but looking more closely you notice lines have been roughly scratched into some of the items. You wonder . . . perhaps a final message?

▶ *Follow the second letter of the message to the next passage.*

Blink

You cut the wires, push open the door, and rush toward the central panel in the lighthouse control room. It only takes a moment to work out how to turn off the light. You count for a few seconds, then switch it back on.

You take a deep breath and feel relief course through your body. Sink to the floor. You're one step closer to the mainland, the evidence, and stopping the bill. All is silent. You close your eyes. Sixty seconds, you tell yourself. Knowing someone is coming to meet you in the bay—that rescue is imminent—makes you rest a little easier.

▶ *Turn to 43.*

79 A Close Shave

Pulling out the map from your pants, you identify 79 as the inmate barber shop.

"Any books, Gennaro?" You ask the barber. He shakes his head. "I want a haircut," you say.

"I'm not expecting," he says. "Too late. Cleaning up."

You try a new approach. You think back to the mess hall earlier on. You say: "ROBIN."

His face lights up. "Gio, buona sera," Gennaro says. And he slips you a package. "No need for clues no more, take this. You follow Holy Word."

"What's goin' on?" Brutal officer "Mac" Robertson blows in. Never lifts his feet, always walks with a shuffle. You turn away and slip the package down the front of your pants. "What're you doin', boy?"

You improvise. Hand Gennaro a copy of Dashiell Hammett's *Red Harvest* actually sent by Jean-Louis to someone in C Block. "Sent from the library. On my way."

Seems Robertson didn't see you conceal the package. You risk a wink at Gennaro.

"You get the numbers out." He thinks you're Gio. That's OK. And Gio is in D Block Solitary. Safely locked away.

You get away as quick as you can with the book trolley. A prisoner in the C Block is waiting for *Red Harvest*.

▶ *Turn to 46.*

Warning Bells

You snip the yellow, blue, and red wires and reach to push open the door. An alarm blares. You try and shut the door behind you to stop it, but no dice.

You decide to try and continue. Maybe you can make it to the shore before anyone notices? You turn off the lighthouse lamp, flash it on again, then rush out of the door and head down, taking the steps two at a time.

But when you reach the bottom of the stairs there's Officer Jorgensen waiting for you.

"Wilson?" he says. He recognizes you despite your guard's uniform and glasses. "I don't believe it. Get down here," he says. "I'm taking you on a little trip to Solitary."

▶ *Turn to 62.*

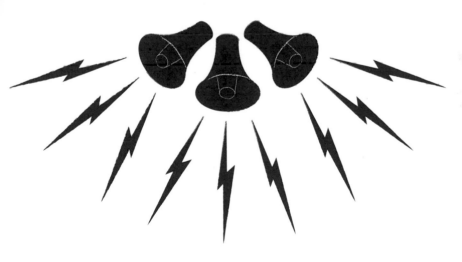

81 Life or Death, Now

FROM 70

Recreation yard. You climb to the top of the steps. You can see the city. The sun on the water. Hills beyond. The beautiful world. Got to get out.

You're making progress. You've cracked the bird books. You have a whole plan laid out for you if you can get to the outer offices. Looks like the Conte crew gave you a tool to pick a lock. Which door?

You think back, try to remember all the things that have been said to you. The map . . . an idea sparks.

Then there are ideas generating in your head from Morris, the Anglins, and West. You have everything you need to get to the offices, at least. Down below, a brawl breaks out. Big Lars pulls out a shiv and tries to cut Ricci. All hell breaks loose. The bulls pile in.

But in the mess hall your optimism evaporates. Conte is talking animatedly to Soprano. The guards are shouting, but you hear him say something like "still here," "no Gio."

Gennaro gave you what you needed to get out. And they expected you to make your move last night. So now they're suspicious that you're not Gio, which explains their angry looks and gestures. Soprano eyeballs you, draws a finger across his throat, smiling broadly, horribly.

It's life or death now. You have to make a move to get out. Away from these animals. Ready or not. Tonight.

▶ *Turn to 89.*

Sing Sing

You edge your way down the rocky cliff and into the Sing Sing cave. Despite its closeness to the water, the cave is warm and dry. You lift the raft off your back. As you do, you're hit with a wave of drowsiness.

"Concentrate," says a voice in your head. At this point you're not quite sure if it's yours or Alison's.

You feel along a sandy shelf at one side of the cave and, after a few minutes, find something cold and hard—metal. You bring down a small, portable safe. It's heavy and sturdy with a circular dial on the front. You spin the dial and it clicks. The clicks feel familiar. You're not quite sure why, or what they remind you of?

You think that the code to this safe is stored in your brain, somewhere. Casting your mind back to meetings with the Wilderness, you decide to trust your gut.

▶ *Add the four digits of the code together.
Turn to the page with that number.*

Vacuum motor. Another nugget of information. You ponder
Huckleberry Finn, looking for clues, connections . . . there is Huck
and Jim finding a raft and a boat?

There's no doubt Morris is up to something, and it seems to be to do
with staying dry . . . or staying afloat?

But back to the Garden puzzle you're sure is associated with Birdman
and his escape plot. A view through a window will have to do—and so,
consulting your map, you steer the book trolley to the library.

You find a window you believe will offer a good vantage point and
climb up onto the trolley to look out. It takes a moment to identify the
part of the garden Birdman's note indicated.

You expect multicolored blooms in red, pink, and yellow, but find yourself instead peering mainly at piles of dirt.

Badum, badum. You can hear your heartbeat in your ears.

"With no flowers, how will I know which color to pick?" you ask no one. But Alison's voice responds. "Birdman's note," she whispers, her voice in rhythm with your thumping heart.

You reach into your pocket and pull out Birdman's scrawled note. Looking closely, you consider the rules:
There are only three colors—red, yellow, pink.
No flowers can border a patch with the same color.
The cogs in your head start to turn.

▶ Use the code wheel to follow the first letter of the color you choose.

84 Stroud, R.

Jean-Louis calls. You hurry across the library with the trolley. "Got the first book," you say.

"I saw someone had requested that," he says. "Very odd. You know who Stroud, R. is?"

A pause. You will him to say more.

"Robert Stroud. You heard of him? They called him the Birdman of Alcatraz, though he actually kept birds and wrote about them in his previous prison, Leavenworth.

"Not many left who knew him, 'cept one guard, name of Pierce, was on good terms. He works outside the main block, in the lighthouse, round there. Old now, forgetful . . . But the Governor protects him. Keeps him in work.

"Anyways, Pierce told me there was a rumor Stroud was cooking up an escape plan involving keys and codes to the outer offices. Stroud was a fan of brainteasers, and it seems he got into crafting them himself. Once or twice I've looked at books he borrowed and come across these scribblings—but I can't make head nor tail of them.

"Nothing was ever carried through, anyway. He was transferred out due to sickness . . ."

His voice trails off. Has he spotted the seven books you have piled on the trolley? You look at him as steadily as you can. He recollects himself, but gives you a strange smile. You open your mouth to speak, but Jean-Louis walks away.

▶ *Turn to 4.*

Treasure Island

You push off toward Treasure Island. San Francisco glimmers in the dawn light. You feel a great sense of ease.

When you reach what you believe to be the meeting point you bring yourself to a stop. You bob there for a few moments, then a few moments more.

Minutes turn to hours, and soon you're under a midday sun. It dawns on you that you must, somehow, have got something wrong.

You manage to keep the evidence dry. In the early afternoon, the Coast Guard pulls up beside you and, on noticing your clothes, immediately takes you back to The Rock. The evidence weighs heavy in your pocket and on your mind.

▶ *Turn to 38.*

Symbol N

You're sure that 🦉 fits in the bottom-center spot. You look eagerly around for it. But . . . maybe you misread the puzzle? Panic is never far from the surface in here. You are breathless and can feel your heart racing. You return to the board and try again.

▶ *Turn back to 27.*

87 The Mail

The next morning you are relieved that after breakfast you're directed back to the library. You arrive to see Jean-Louis reorganizing the magazine section.

"Lot of interest in *Popular Mechanics* and *Sports Illustrated*," he says. "Curious." You scan the room. On the long table, some clippings from the *San Francisco Mail* catch your eye.

Something in your lost memory chimes. This paper . . . was connected somehow to the Wilderness plot.

Jean-Louis notices your interest. "Newspaper cuttings are like gold dust in Alcatraz. They try to keep inmates isolated from the outside world. I think it would be better to let people know what's goin' on . . . With our fine young president . . . and what they're calling the Space Race."

The headline strikes you: "LAND LOBBY BILL: 3 DAYS TO DECIDE FUTURE." Could this have been the bill you dreamed about? The bill is to push through the sale of a huge expanse of land to agricultural businesses, and there's a challenge by Indigenous activists. This is BIG. On the reverse of the torn piece of newspaper, a classified ad grabs your eye:

> Lighthouse Island Soon Travel Enabled. Now Understand Paper Shows Crafty Operation Together Together

You read it again, and again something chimes in your brain. Is this a message, a coded communication?

▶ *You find the hidden message, turn to 74.*

▶ *You can't decipher it, turn to 2.*

"Oh Boy"

Room 9, the Birdman's step 4, is the storage room. Inside you find a corner rack full of guard uniforms. Genius! You marvel at ol' Robert's planning. You find a uniform that fits, change into it. There is a looking glass and you check yourself out in it. Not bad, but still recognizable?

For good measure you take a hat and some eyeglasses someone has put down. They look like Officer Washington's. Or like Buddy Holly, you think sadly. What a tragedy that was. Lenses are mild—you can see okay.

All the time you're lugging with you the heavy raft that Morris, West, and the Anglins made. You're tempted to dump it, but you know you'll need it later.

In the projection room you search for—and find—a green key, step 5 of Stroud's plan. The next step is room 7. You see it—the projection room. It's unlocked. But inside are locked windows. Your heart in your mouth, you try the green key. It works! The window opens with a squeak.

You stand still, peering out—no sign of any guards. You see a manageable way down across the roof to a drainpipe—and to the ground . . .

Oh boy. You clamber out and across the roof. You feel like singing, and do, under your breath . . . "Tonight there'll be no hesitatin', oh boy . . ."

You look up at the sky. "Stars appear and shadows fallin', You can hear my heart callin'. . ." You're out. Safe on the ground. But you still have to find the package you're looking for—and get off The Rock.

▶ *Turn to 73.*

89 A Lifeline

You rush back to the library, knowing you only have a few moments to find the message you need. That's assuming the paper is even here.

Your eyes dart around the room when you arrive, and you breathe a sigh of relief when you notice some clippings in the trash. You flick straight to the ads and scan down quickly to find the message you're looking for.

> XKKN MN QFXK WAFZN QFUSNSAOYK.
> Bring the treasure with you. Let's hope the angels are looking down on us.

▶ *Turn to 66.*

Deciphered Dreams

You think back through your dreams and try to unpick the messages they contained: from cryptic sentences to a sung scene, and from confused physics to being trapped in a safe.

You ponder your next move.

▶ *To go to Sing Sing cave and look for the evidence on a shelf, turn to 82.*

▶ *To go to San Antonio cave and look for the evidence in a hole, turn to 56.*

▶ *To go to the wharf and look for the evidence on a roof, turn to 29.*

No Problem

Your hand reaches for an end of rope. You pull and wind the rope that follows into a neat pile. You look across at the guard, Svenson.

He nods and you get some more ropes to sort.

Soon it is time for the recreation yard. A group of men are driven there by Svenson and Minnelli.

▶ *Turn to 41.*

Jorgensen leads you down the central corridor between tables. All the tables are full. You keep walking, stumble once, pushed from behind by Minnelli. Until, down the end, you find a table empty along the near side.

"You're lucky, boy," Jorgensen says, emphasizing words with a sneer in his voice. "You get to dine with our most elite guests . . ." Then he barks: "What are you boys doing?" You notice some commotion at the tables. Some of the men nearby are standing and seem to be moving glasses and cutlery. "Sit down, Conte!" he barks. He's addressing one of the group who is standing over by the radiator.

He says, "Filippo Conte, New York." Bows. "We welcome the fresh fish. Save a place. Take account where you goin'."

He waves a hand at the tables nearby—"Soprano, Ricci." Conte swings his arm across the table. "Hundreds of us in here," he says, pointing toward the left-hand side of the window, before dropping his hand to the table.

Puzzled and unsure if you're being greeted or threatened, you nod your head to Conte. "Thanks."

"No talking!" Jorgensen shouts and bangs the table.

Before you sit you take in the scene. Something's definitely odd about the way the men are standing and how everything's arranged on the tables. You take careful note.

▶ *Follow the number you find.*

Exhausted. Music Hour. Slumped on your bed, you close your eyes. In the next cell Morris is playing Acker Bilk's hit "Stranger on the Shore" on his accordion.

Music reminds you of the message you decoded from the tapping on the water pipes. And the magazine you picked up, an issue of *Popular Mechanics*. Dated March, 1962.

Odd choice for cons to be passing around. If that's what happened . . . You look inside the magazine for clues or leads. Inside the cover on the contents page beneath the word PAGE you find a number puzzle in tiny handwriting.

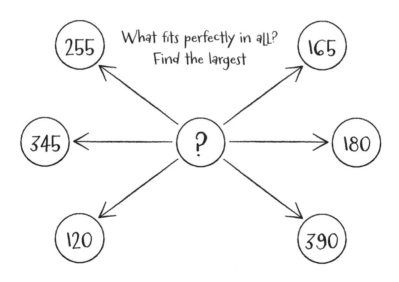

▶ *Work out the missing number and turn to that passage.*

Alpha and Omega

You're out! But not really. You feel like shouting for joy but there are many stages to this plan, and each one demands calm and care.

You have the tool Gennaro gave you. It is wrapped in a piece of paper, with a handwritten sentence from the Bible's Book of Revelation. One word is underlined. There are also some shapes with numbers.

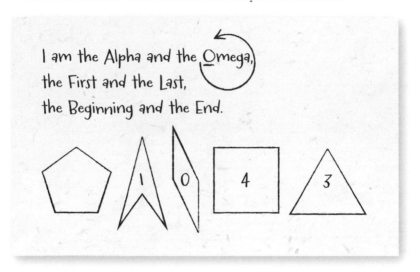

Alpha to Omega, you think. First to last. And the Bible passage . . . you glance at the map and note the stairs to the chapel, remember the words: "the last place you should try"—that must be it.

You know guards are on patrol, but you're safely out of sight where you are. Patience. You wait while a guard shuffles past. Robertson? From the end of the elevated utility corridor, you shimmy down a pipe to the floor of the prison block and across to the door. The last place.

You gently insert the tool in the lock, but how many turns, and which way? You glance again at the note: the underlined Omega, the small arrow around it, and the shapes.

▶ *Follow the code wheel to the correct answer.*

95 Wool

You finish calculating and hesitantly land on "WOOL." As you're beginning to stand, you notice the other Gio standing, too. He's not walking toward "WOOL," but veering uncertainly in another direction, toward either "PINS" or "CALF." But then he returns to his seat, scratching his balding head. You also slide back into your seat. You look back at the fabric and the pins and calculate again.

▶ Turn back to 5.

96 Grim Reading

It could be minutes or hours later. The door is wrenched open. The light is dazzling, pouring into the cell. It's Officer Beckett.

"Mornin' Wilson. Just enjoying my newspaper here." He smirks as he shows you the page. How does he know you were connected to the land deal? Then your eye falls on the small story about Jean-Louis.

Beckett wants you to read it. He's giving you time to do it.

"Communist anti-business group." You snort. But you wonder if you could feel any lower.

The End

SAN FRANCISCO MAIL

LAND DEAL AGREED

WILDERNESS MADE SAFE

FARMERS' SPOKESMAN: "FUTURE SECURED"
STATE OFFICIAL: "PEOPLE WANT TO BE FED"

The sale of 200,000 acres of northern Californian wilderness to a group of large landowners and farmers has been hailed as a triumph by the farmers' group spokesman. Mr. Wiley W. Harrison, Jr., said that the deal would secure the future of the land and ensure that it did not "fall into the wrong hands." He stressed what a great resource the land is for the state, and the need to use "all that modern science can deliver" to maximize its productivity.

Mr. Harrison's associate Dr. Karl "Chuck" Boschwitz, referring to protests from members of anti-pesticide groups, said: "I call those fellas anti-farmers. This is a good day, a great moment for California. We'll make those acres pay."

A police spokesman told the Mail, "We were on hand, allowing us to eliminate a protest being planned against this important deal. Wrongdoers have been rounded up and face long sentences in some of our least hospitable institutions. So they'll have plenty of time to see the error of their ways and let's pray they live to experience the benefits of this agreement."

Continued on page 2

PRISONER FACING MORE TIME

Alcatraz inmate and librarian Jean-Louis Lévesque was arrested Monday accused of involvement with communist anti-business group the Wilderness, and also with attempting to help a fellow prisoner escape .

Continued on page 3.

DEADLY "SILENT SPRING"

The Mail has seen an advance copy of marine biologist Rachel Carson's potentially sensational new book Silent Spring, due to be published this fall. It warns of the dangers of pesticides' poisonous effect on the environment.

Continued on page 31

FRANNY AND ZOOEY TOP OF THE PILE

JD Salinger's novel Franny and Zooey, one of the top-selling novels of 1961, remains at the top of the most-wanted lists in our bookstores.

Continued on page 7

TRIBAL COUNCIL APPROVES ELVIS ROLE

Elvis Presley has been inducted into the Los Angeles Tribal Council by Wah-Nee-Ota after the success of the King's role in Flaming Star, which opened just before Christmas.

Continued on page 12

You're grateful to get back to the library. You'd hoped that you were back to full health, but even a short stint of wheeling the book trolley has taken it out of you.

The library is empty when you arrive, and you take the opportunity to sink into the chair in front of Jean-Louis's desk and get a moment of rest. You glance at an open drawer and spy a few clippings from the *San Francisco Mail*. You can't quite believe your luck. Jean-Louis can't have known? Right?

You flick the paper open to the letters section and scan for anything conspicuous. You're surprised by how quickly you find it:

---

am bv mxwc qerdsy gu hsifzj cp dbjl kg nzoa uovr yt ektn xi lqfh pw

Esolc daer. Worromot semoc noitacol. Ydaer nehw. Knilb. Lla sees esuohthgil eht.

▶ *Turn to 21.*

An Ally?

As Jean-Louis makes his way across the room you stash the books on the ornithology shelves. Jean-Louis looks at you, eyebrows raised.

He is staring at your arm. You realize your arm tattoo is visible after you rolled up your sleeves.

"That looks . . . familiar?"

You look at him.

"The WILDERNESS?" he says. "Are you connected?"

You briefly describe the raid, being framed—and jailed.

He drops his voice to a whisper. "Incredible. I'm a supporter—from afar. I—I believe in your work. That case I heard from a contact, the bill that is, what you're doing is so important . . ."

He looks at you almost in awe. You're about to tell him about the cell block map in the book, ask him if he thinks it's connected, but he gestures at you silently and leaves the room.

▶ _Turn to 30._

You know events are pressing. To hell with taking your time. You need to get your head in gear, but you took a heavy blow and you spend the day drifting in and out of consciousness. The sun slowly sets outside the window. Each time you wake your head feels a little clearer.

A nurse walks over to your bed. "Wilson," he says, looking at your chart. "We'll have to keep you overnight. You need to be monitored."

You try to nod, but your head can't move. He continues: "The librarian dropped this off for you." He places a book on your bedside table and walks away. It's another from the ornithology section: *Birds: A Guide to the Most Familiar American Birds*, by Herbert Zim. And you note it has another of Birdman's symbols on the spine ⟨⟩.

Tucked into the front cover is a handwritten note from Jean-Louis. "Sorry to hear of your fall." On the back: "Birdman spent a lot of time in the infirmary. This was one of his favorites while he was there, I believe. I hope it gives you some solace. J-L."

You flick through the book's pages. It's a comprehensive overview of the country's birds. But that's not what you're looking for. On the final page you find something. A handwritten grid, covered in circles and arrows. There is a short instruction.

Each row, column, and box will feature the numbers 1–9 once. The numbers in the circles are the same as the total of the numbers along the attached arrows. Follow the red.

You look at the grid. Your concussion-addled brain tries to keep up. The number placement seems easy enough, but "follow the red"— what can that mean?

You shuffle in your bedsheets and then your eyes are caught by the shelves directly opposite your bed. The layout is the same as the grid. Some have bottles of medicine, others have bandages. The shelves are a 9 x 9 square and in some of the holes there are letters. And one hole is painted red.

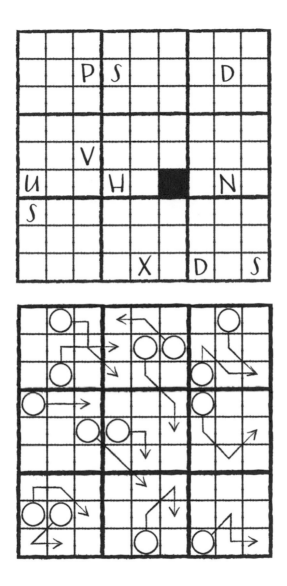

You compare the sketch and the shelves and your brain spins into action.

▶ *Follow the red square.*

After settling into Cell 138 you lie right down and fall asleep. But not for long. Hours are ticking down till that land deal goes through . . . You check out the books. You've got *A Field Guide to the Birds of Britain and Europe* by Petersen 🐦 and *Menaboni's Birds* by Athos and Sara Menaboni. 🦉. Yawn.

Both have a Birdman symbol marked on the cover, but you struggle to find anything inside. You can't quite work out if it's the dull nature of the books, your drowsy brain, or an added layer of difficulty, but it takes you what feels like hours to find the first hint of a message.

Slowly, you piece it together—another puzzle. In the Petersen book, drawn onto the back of one of the pages, is a sequence of cards, in a tower. The card at the top is turned down.

A message reads underneath. "Follow the pattern, find the top card." You push your brain into gear.

▶ *Follow the number you find.*

Angel Island

You navigate toward Angel Island. You breathe a sigh of relief and let yourself imagine your first few hours back in San Francisco, a grilled cheese and a cold beer. You reach what you believe to be the pick-up point and stop.

You think of nothing but the grilled cheese for the first few minutes. But then these minutes turn into hours. The grilled cheese moves further and further away.

At about midday, despite your best efforts to paddle away, you're picked up by the Coast Guard. They sigh, and shake their heads, and take you straight back to Alcatraz.

▶ *Turn to 38.*

102 In Knots

FROM 65

After breakfast, and several strong cups of joe, you're pushed roughly to your first labor detail.

Your dream still hangs around you, and in it you feel the gaps. All that you can't remember. You know that the events of the night of the raid are in your mind, somewhere, but between the gunshots, the screams, and the harsh blow to your head, they've slipped away.

You're marched by a new guard, Svenson, into a large warehouse, deposited at a table, and a mound of rope is placed in front of you. The guard barks a single word:

"Sort!"

You look at the three piles of rope, and pick up one of the loose ends. Put it down again. You're not sure how to "sort." You glance around at the other tables, but are careful not to look too long. Being caught staring is going to leave you with nothing but a black eye. You consider the mound of rope and ponder your next step.

You decide the best course of action is to pull at one end of the rope and hope that it'll unspool in front of you. But you're not quite sure where to begin, and how to avoid pulling the rope into a knotty mess.

Which clump of rope below has no knots?

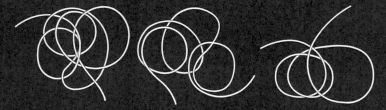

▶ *If you think it's A, turn to 52.*
▶ *If you think it's B, turn to 91.*
▶ *If you think it's C, turn to 63.*

You work out the answer—103—but you're not sure what to make of it. After the meal Minnelli and Jorgensen drive you all like cattle back to your cells. A few men from the dining table are muttering.

". . . and that's why he cannot make himself known?"

"It's a command from NYC. We have to find out which one. We get it wrong, big trouble. So, we make some tests . . ."

You follow the guards. At Times Square, Minnelli screams: "Broadway residences!" Each prisoner stands outside his cell. You keep an eye on who is going where. At 107 you see Ricci. At 115 you see Michelangelo. At 103 you see Conte.

You don't get a chance to see who else is on Broadway, as Jorgensen starts to herd you and a crowd of other men to Michigan Avenue. When each prisoner is outside his own cell, the doors are all opened at once with a lever device. In you go.

You sink onto your bed. The worst day of your life. But your luck must change. Something a Wilderness colleague, Alison, said comes back. You make your own luck. Perhaps she's right. Poor Alison, shot dead in the raid.

You lie down in your day clothes, trying to make a mental note of what you've picked up. The Bible page with its message. The newspaper column about the Mafia accountant Gio. The information the men seemed to be communicating in the mess hall. The murmurs you overheard . . . were they talking about this "Gio"? You commit names and cell numbers to memory. Is there a link? Sleep and dreams sweep over you.

▶ *Turn to 65.*

104 A Flock of Books

Jorgensen looks daggers at you as he escorts you to the library. On the library table you find a note of the books requested by the inmates. Jean-Louis is not here now but has clearly been in already today.

Is something wrong with the heating? It's warm. You roll up your sleeves as far as they will go. You review the list and to find the first book you wander over to OR: Ornithology. This must be where Jean-Louis got the book he gave you yesterday. And come to think of it, as you look around you note other symbols on the covers of books scattered all over the shelves.

You put down the book Jean-Louis gave you yesterday, *Birds of the World*, on a table.

You catch yourself for a moment. What are you doing? Finding books? Solving riddles? You're locked in Alcatraz for a crime you didn't commit, and you desperately need to escape. The Wilderness, whatever is left of them, needs you.

You run through your options. A prison break is a no-go. You're a strong swimmer but there's no way you'd make it from the island, you're sure. Claiming your innocence does nothing either. This seems to be the only route, even if it is rather roundabout.

You flick your eyes back to the shelves and review the books scattered across them.

▶ *Add all the symbols you find and turn to the corresponding passage.*

HINTS & SOLUTIONS FOR INMATES

Hints

1 — Cell 136
Perhaps the three sticks of chalk (taken back) are
meant as a clue for interpreting the passage.

5 — Fine Tailoring
Is there anything already in some corners to help you?

8 — Snake Eyes
What does one total needing to be half the other tell
you? Be quick—the sands of time are running out!

12 — Annotations
What's missing?

17 — Evidence
The scrambled messages in the San Francisco Mail might
unscramble to lead the way. To help, look at what came
before. It might offer you a lifeline.

18 — "Do the Twist"
What might the dots and dashes be?

19 — A Musical Vision
It might be worth taking some notes on last
night's dream.

22 — Huckleberry Finn
Where could the page numbers lead you?

26 — Back on Broadway
Can you spot a sequence in symbols? What reason could
Conte have for pointing out the headline of the review
he's reading?

27 — In the Books
Focus on a side and compare it with others. Top and
bottom are good places to start.

32 — What's Cooking?
What does it mean for something to be true?

34 — Prison Hospital
It's worth keeping a note of this dream—it might be
important later.

35 — Tree of Letters
What names do you find in a bird handbook?

41 — In the Recreation Yard
Breaks in the fence might leave you dotty but don't dash
your hopes of escape . . .

42 — Cell 138
Look more closely beneath the sink.

43 — The Right Frequency
Take a note of this dream—some details might be
important later.

47 — Silent Night
Always be alert—what's missing? Where to begin?

48 — A Librarian's Code
Librarians care about where it all begins, but they're
aware that sometimes names move.

50 — Deep Dreams
Some details of your dream might be important later.

54 — Cards
The grays might be more helpful than you think.

59 — The Warden
Only connect—what might the framed pictures be
referencing? And how might this combine with the
imprinted message on the table?

60 — Step by Step
The first three numbers are in the top two levels.

66 — The Dead of Night
What did you see in Morris's cell that might show you where to go here?

68 — Dominoes
Some pairs only appear once. Can these show you the way?

69 — Corner Shelves
Can you triangulate your way to an answer?

73 — The Lighthouse
Follow the note and focus on the lighthouse. What might the visuals represent?

"X" marks the spot, and what else?

77 — Mealtime
If you think of the lines as numbers, consider how you can combine numbers and the names of objects.

82 — Sing Sing
Your dreams have led you here—might they show you how to open the safe too? What might the clicks have reminded you of?

83 — The Garden
Look closely. Start with what you know. Which flowers can be planted in the empty spots?

87 — The Mail
It's often useful to start at the beginning.

89 — A Lifeline
What have the previous messages from the Mail told you? Could the pairs of letters from yesterday's paper help? If M means A, what could the jumble reveal?

90 — Deciphered Dreams
What have your dreams been trying to tell you?

92 — Mess Hall
Why did Conte say "Hundreds of us in here" while pointing at the glass on the furthest left of that window? Count up what you think with your digits.

93 — Popular Mechanics
What does it mean when one number fits perfectly into another?

94 — Alpha and Omega
Reflect carefully on this one. You should find yourself looking back. Then start with Omega, and let it take you for a spin.

97 — Message in the Mail
Most people read messages forward but you're not most people.

99 — A Book to Read
How can you convert the letters to numbers? To start solving, think about what each square could be, and eliminate from there.

100 — A Long Night
Can you treat the suits and values as two different sequences?

102 — In Knots
Try and trace the pattern from one end to another. If you have to twist around another piece of rope, you've found a knot.

104 — A Flock of Books
A pair of sharp eyes and a spin of the code wheel will help you here.

Solutions

1 — Cell 136
The trick is to take the third letter before each circled letter. This spells "Benvenuto Gio," meaning "Welcome Gio," in Italian. The third letter of the message is "n" and its place in the alphabet is 14. Turn to 14.

5 — Fine Tailoring
Consider the number 7. This sits in the intersection of a triangle and a square, and represents the total number of corners present in both shapes. The 9, too, is the intersection of a square and a pentagon—that is 9 corners in total.

Now if we look at the pins:
• One is the intersection of a pentagon and a square: 9
• One is the intersection of a triangle, hexagon, and a square: 13
• One is the intersection of 2 pentagons, a hexagon, a square, and a triangle: 23
• One is the intersection of 2 squares, 2 triangles, and a hexagon: 20
We put these into the code wheel to get letters: "F—L—C—A." Which we can rearrange to spell "CALF." Turn to 76.

8 — Snake Eyes
This is the correct configuration. The red lines (of 3) add to 8, while the blue lines (of 5) add to 16.

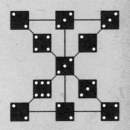

The shorter lines add to 8. The code wheel reveals "u" as 2, so 8 minus 2 gives you 6. Turn to 6.

12 — Annotations
There are blacked-out places where letters are missing: The letter "n" is missing from "morning."

The letter "i" is missing from "lying."
The letter "o" is missing from "some."
The letter "t" is missing from "the."
The letter "a" is missing from "damp."
The letter "a" is missing from "bare."
The letter "c" is missing from "coarser."
The letter "r" is missing from "spider."

This gives you "n, i, o, t, a, a, c, r," which, unscrambled, spells "raincoat."

17 — Evidence
Head for the Lime Point Lighthouse. This message was written in the last Mail article (89), using a substitution cipher, where the letters of the alphabet were moved around. The key for this was written into the previous day's article (97).

18 — "Do the Twist"
You use Morse code to translate the dots and dashes into letters and numbers, and reveal the message: POPMEC362. You note it down for future use.

22 — Huckleberry Finn
The numbers of the loose pages indicate letters in the dedication. They spell out "vacuum motor." This must be some piece of equipment needed for the escape plan, you decide.

25 — Hospital Reading
Knowing that it is a common sign of mental disturbance to have delusions of being someone famous such as Elvis or Jesus, you are pretending to be Napoleon exiled on St. Helena—another man stuck on a rock surrounded by waves. Mr. Willam Balcombe was Napoleon's host. You're trying to prolong your stay in the hospital and stave off the impending threat of solitary confinement by pretending to be deranged.

26 — Back on Broadway

The symbols represent a descending sequence of prime numbers. And the arrow on the floor suggests you should progress the sequence to find your next destination. The magazine headline, underlined by Conte's chatter, alert you to consider prime numbers. The second and third numbers can be obtained from the code wheel, giving you 97—89—83—? The next prime in the sequence is 79. Turn to 79.

27 — In the Books

The bottom-center symbol is 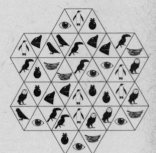. Turn to 10.

32 — What's Cooking?

The only circumstance where two statements are true and one is a lie is where:
F is true;
Y is true;
O is false.

This means O is not poison, and then because Y is true, this makes F poison.

Putting F into the code wheel gives green so you go through the green door. Turn to 28.

35 — Tree of Letters

The words can be found in the leaves as follows:
1. BALD EAGLE (GO NATIONAL)
2. CROW (HOARSE BLACK)
3. CARDINAL (RED CRESTED)
4. CANARY (CAGED YELLOW)

This leaves a leftover "a," which sends you to passage 20.

41 — In the Recreation Yard

You need to look in the library. The dots (knots) and dashes (gaps) in the fence spell out these letters in Morse code: "B—I—L." Reversing them you get "L—I—B," which indicates the library.

· — ·· L

·· I

— · · · B

If you add the places in the alphabet of "L" (12), "I" (9), and "B" (2) you get 23. Turn to 23.

42 — Cell 138

You notice a few things in Morris's cell that provide important clues as to how he and his associates the Anglin brothers and Allen West are progressing the escape plan you heard them mentioning. They seem to be accessing an opening beneath the sink. Where could that lead? You look on your map and identify the utility corridor (number 33 on map) running behind the cells. You guess they are working on their escape plan in the corridor. You might think back to the song Morris was singing during Music Hour—to the idea of twisting (a tool) and twisting (through the hole in the wall).

47 — Silent Night

"Always be Alert" contains the letters "W," "Y," "B," and "R" suggesting that the white, yellow, blue, and red wires should stay. The letters "G," "O," and "P" aren't present in the message, suggesting these wires should be cut. Turn to 78.

48 — A Librarian's Code

For each book, the cell numbers are reversed, and then placed at the start of the code. Then the first letter of the book's title and the first letter of the author's surname are put through a Caesar shift cipher, which moves the letter 14 places. This was indicated by Jean-Louis' "14."

This matches up:
1. Hank Mortensen, Cell 245 to **A Raisin in the Sun**,
Lorraine Hansberry
2. Filippo Conte, Cell 103, to **Rebecca**, Daphne
du Maurier
3. Frank Morris, Cell 138, to **Catch-22**, Joseph Heller
4. Aaron Johnson, Cell 127, to **Notes of a Native Son**,
James Baldwin

Notes of a Native Son should be delivered to
Aaron Johnson, Cell 127. The first two digits of this
number are 12. Turn to passage 12.

54 — Cards
"K" is the value in the
middle. Using the code
wheel directs you to 22.
Turn to 22.

59 — The Warden
The answer is 36, the total number of plays William
Shakespeare wrote that appeared in the First Folio. The
clues around the warden's office indicate his passion:

A bear for **The Winter's Tale**
A dagger in red for **Romeo and Juliet**
A skull with a crown for **Hamlet**

The message on the desk, imprinted, reads
"FF Plays," leading you to the number 36.
Turn to 36.

60 — Step by Step
The correct arrangement is shown.

Follow the red triangle. Turn to 8.

66 — The Dead of Night
In Cell 138 you saw a ventilation panel loose
underneath the sink. This leads to the utility corridor,
which you can see from your map. Turn to 33.

68 — Dominoes
The domino totals are:
Top left: 6
Top right: 8
Bottom left: 11
Bottom right: 6
These add to 31. Turn to 31.

2	0	3	2	3	1	4	4
4	2	2	3	6	1	2	6
0	6	0	2	2	5	1	0
1	5	5	0	4	6	5	0
3	3	1	5	6	3	1	2
5	5	6	0	6	4	3	1
6	4	5	4	0	1	3	5

69 — Corner Shelves
The answer is 🔔. Then each
triangle of six circles,
whichever way up, contains
one example of one shape,
two of another, and three
of a third. Neat.

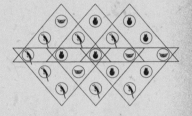

Using the code wheel you can identify the missing
symbol with the number 16. Turn to 16.

73 — The Lighthouse
Each visual on the note relates to an architectural
feature on the lighthouse:
The octagons to the octagon shapes at the top of the
lighthouse (on the building and fence)—there are 5.
The circle to the circular platform at the top—there
is 1.
The bar to the lines down the body of the lighthouse—
there are 8.

The "x," as well as marking the spot to stand, also
indicates you should multiply the numbers together.
Doing this you get: 5 x 8 x 1 = 40. Turn to 40.

77 — Mealtime
The lines direct you to the letter of the alphabet you should take from the name of that object.
Fork—3 lines = "R"
Spoon—3 lines = "O"
Bowl—1 line = "B"
Pitcher—2 lines = "I"
Spoon—5 lines = "N"

"O" is the second letter of the message and corresponds to 26 on the code wheel. Turn to 26.

82 - Sing Sing
Your final dream "The Right Frequency" suggested to you that the evidence is in a safe, but in fact an indication of the safe has been in every dream.

There were 3 clicks in "Deep Dreams" (50)
There were 7 clicks in "A Musical Vision" (19)
There was 1 click in "Prison Hospital" (34)
There were 6 clicks in "The Right Frequency" (43)

This is the code for the safe—3-7-1-6—added together, giving you 17. Turn to 17.

83 — The Garden
The two patches with both red and yellow divided by a white line could have either color flower and both answers are correct.

The bird is on a yellow patch. "Y" is the first letter and corresponds to 19 on the code wheel. Turn to 19.

87 — The Mail
Taking the first letter from each word gives us a
message L-I-S-T-E-N U-P S-C-O-T-T.

89 — A Lifeline
The message is decoded using a substitution cipher,
where each letter is replaced by another. In the
previous message (97) after it was reversed, letter pairs
indicated what substitutions to make:

wp hfql ntke ty rvou aozn gk ljbd pc jzfish ug ysdreq
cwxm vb ma

For example, the first pair in the reversed message are
"wp," meaning replace "w" with "p."

Decoded it reads: "Meet at Lime Point Lighthouse." You
save this information for later.

90 — Deciphered Dreams
Go to Sing Sing and look for something on the shelf.
This was told to you in your dreams.

In "Deep Dreams" (50), each sentence spoken to you had
words beginning with "C-A-V-E," suggesting you should
go to a cave.

In "A Musical Vision" (19), everyone was singing, sending
you to SING SING. This was further indicated by the map
compass spelling out: "S-I-N-G."

In "Prison Hospital" (34), everyone was reaching up,
indicating the evidence is on a shelf.

Turn to 82.

92 — Mess Hall
Conte means to alert you that your task is to identify
this as a calculation that holds a clue about a

location that might become important. The three glasses
set against the window frame indicate 111. This is why
Conte said "Hundreds" while pointing at the glass on
the far left.

The horizontal spoon on the table is a minus sign.
Collectively the men in the scene are showing
eight fingers.
Two horizontal forks is an equals sign.

111 - 8 = 103.

The answer is 103. For your next clue you need to look
out for any leads associated with the number 103. Turn
to 103.

93 — Popular Mechanics
The puzzle is asking for the largest number that
divides perfectly into all the others. The answer is 15.
Turn to 15.

94 — Alpha and Omega
The missing number is 5. The numbers refer to the
number of axes of symmetry for each shape. The shape
with the question mark has 5 axes of symmetry.

Alpha and Omega: "Alpha and Omega," the arrow around
Omega, and the underlining of the O can be brought
together to tell you to take the code wheel, starting
at O (the underlining), then turn 5 places (the answer
to the puzzle) counterclockwise (from the arrow). This
gives you 11 on the code wheel. Turn to 11.

97 — Message in the Mail
Read backwards the message says the following:
The lighthouse sees all. Blink. When ready. Location
comes tomorrow. Read close.
wp hfql ntke ty rvou aozn gk ljbd pc jzfish ug ysdreq
cwxm vb ma

You'll need the letters in the second part of the message later.

99 — A Book to Read
The red square is a number 9. Turn to 9.

4	8	1	3	5	6	2	9	7
7	2	3	1	9	8	4	6	5
9	6	5	4	2	7	8	1	3
5	1	4	2	8	3	9	7	6
6	9	8	7	1	4	3	5	2
2	3	7	5	6	9	1	4	8
1	5	6	9	3	2	7	8	4
8	7	2	6	4	1	5	3	9
3	4	9	8	7	5	6	2	1

100 — A Long Night
From top to bottom, left to right the cards go in the following sequence: Hearts—Spades—Diamonds—Clubs.

Each card is the difference between the two below, with 2 added. The top card is a 7 of Hearts. Turn to 7.

102 — In Knots
Image B shows the only piece of string with no knots. Turn to 91.

104 — A Flock of Books
You should get the symbols 👁) ⚷ ⌂ 🐦 ♪ and 🦉. Using the code wheel, to make into numbers, and adding them together, you get: I (17) + R (21) + D (6) + M (18) + A (20) + B (12) + N (4) = 98. (These symbols when converted into letters also spell out "BIRDMAN.") Turn to 98.

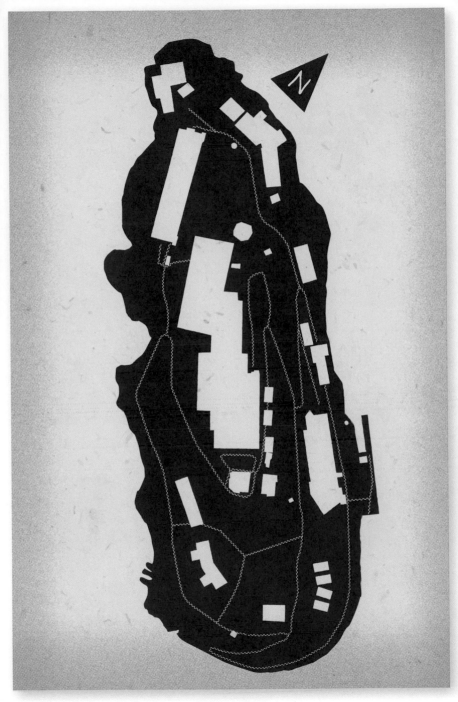

THE ALCATRAZ ESCAPE BOOK

THE ROCK

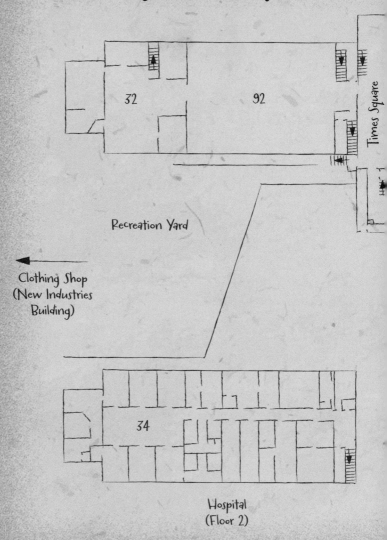

32

92

Times Square

Recreation Yard

Clothing Shop
(New Industries
Building)

34

Hospital
(Floor 2)

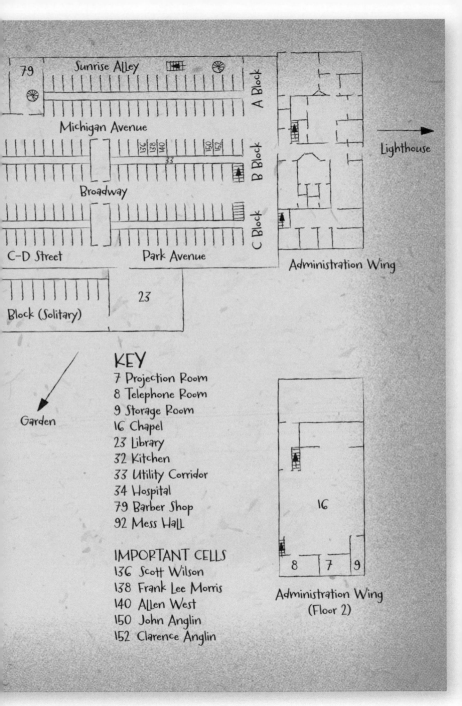

79

Sunrise Alley

A Block

Michigan Avenue

136 138 140   150 152
33

B Block

Broadway

C Block

C-D Street

Park Avenue

Administration Wing

Block (Solitary)

23

Lighthouse

Garden

KEY
7 Projection Room
8 Telephone Room
9 Storage Room
16 Chapel
23 Library
32 Kitchen
33 Utility Corridor
34 Hospital
79 Barber Shop
92 Mess Hall

IMPORTANT CELLS
136 Scott Wilson
138 Frank Lee Morris
140 Allen West
150 John Anglin
152 Clarence Anglin

16

8 7 9

Administration Wing
(Floor 2)

The Liberation of Alcatraz Island:
Native American Occupation of Alcatraz Island and the Reawakening of the Native Spirit

U.S.P. Alcatraz closed in 1963, leading to a very different chapter in the history of the Bay Area—the Occupation of Alcatraz (1969–71). This was one of the most significant benchmarks in the history of the struggle for Native American political sovereignty.

In 1871, Congress ceased recognizing the Native American tribes as independent nations, bringing an end to the genocide and treaty-making period. In the following years, Congress banned Native culture, languages, customs, songs, dances, and ceremonies. One of the most notorious policies was the establishment of government and Christian boarding schools far from the reservations. Native children were taken hostage and sent to them to further ensure non-resistance. The "cycle of dysfunction" that has had a devastating impact on generations of Native Americans began as a direct result of the physical, mental, and sexual abuse of the children, which in turn impacted future generations through historic boarding-school trauma.

In the post-genocidal era of twentieth-century Native America, tribes were fighting many battles against the injustices and discrimination that were results of the colonial government. During the 1950s and 60s, the Bureau of Indian Affairs Relocation Policy intended to "Assimilate Indians into the mainstream of American society" by sending young people into the largest cities of America to speed up the process of colonization. However, this attempt backfired on the government by unwittingly creating a perfect storm for activism, particularly in California universities.

Natives relocated into the San Francisco Bay Area began to work together and organize as identifiable groups in the city's demography. Many of these Native youth decided they wanted professional degrees. San Francisco State and the University of California were magnets for Native students, and many joined other ethnic students to organize and

LaNada was one of the key organizers of the Occupation. During this period, a variety of political messages were painted on the water tower, and the tower is now classed as a cultural landmark. The messages were repainted after the tower was restored in 2011–12.
(Credit: Golden Gate NRA, Park Archives.)

implement their own "Third World Studies," which proved to be highly successful. It was these students who liberated Alcatraz Island in peaceful protest of the government's ill treatment of Native people and broken treaties. The Occupation of Alcatraz was pivotal for taking a stand against the colonial powers and reconnecting with the Native Americans' lost identity, culture, and spirituality.

Dr. LaNada War Jack
President of Indigenous Visions Network
Chair of Indians of All Tribes, Inc.
Member of the Shoshone-Bannock Tribes of the
Fort Hall Indian Reservation in Idaho
www.drwarjack.com

First published 2023 by
Ammonite Press
an imprint of Guild of Master Craftsman Publications Ltd
Castle Place, 166 High Street, Lewes, East Sussex, BN7 1XU,
United Kingdom

ISBN 978-1-78145-478-7

A catalogue record for this book is available from the British Library.

Publisher: Jonathan Bailey
Design Manager: Robin Shields
Senior Project Editor: Tom Kitch
Editor: Robin Pridy

Colour reproduction by GMC Reprographics
Printed and bound in China

The publisher would like to thank John Martini and the staff of Golden Gate N.R.A.
for their advice regarding the layout of U.S.P. Alcatraz. They are not responsible for
any of the content of this book, and any errors are the publisher's.

This is a work of fiction. Although some of the characters are named after real
inmates of Alcatraz, all aspects of their portrayal and any event described in this
book are entirely products of the authors' imaginations. Any resemblance of any
other character in the book (including, but not limited to, any state or federal
employee), to actual persons, living or dead, is purely coincidental.

If you've escaped the pages (or are still
trapped!) please send us a message:
#AlcatrazEscapeBook
@ammonitepress

AMMONITE

www.ammonitepress.com